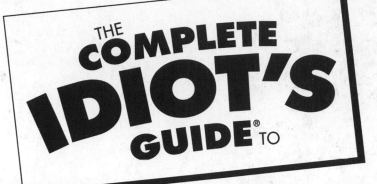

THE COMPLETE IDIOT'S GUIDE® TO

Webkinz®

*by Marcia Layton Turner
and Grant Turner*

ALPHA

A member of Penguin Group (USA) Inc.

For Amanda, owner of Chippy, Eyelash, and Wilbur.

ALPHA BOOKS

Published by the Penguin Group

Penguin Group (USA) Inc., 375 Hudson Street, New York, New York 10014, USA

Penguin Group (Canada), 90 Eglinton Avenue East, Suite 700, Toronto, Ontario M4P 2Y3, Canada (a division of Pearson Penguin Canada Inc.)

Penguin Books Ltd., 80 Strand, London WC2R 0RL, England

Penguin Ireland, 25 St. Stephen's Green, Dublin 2, Ireland (a division of Penguin Books Ltd.)

Penguin Group (Australia), 250 Camberwell Road, Camberwell, Victoria 3124, Australia (a division of Pearson Australia Group Pty. Ltd.)

Penguin Books India Pvt. Ltd., 11 Community Centre, Panchsheel Park, New Delhi—110 017, India

Penguin Group (NZ), 67 Apollo Drive, Rosedale, North Shore, Auckland 1311, New Zealand (a division of Pearson New Zealand Ltd.)

Penguin Books (South Africa) (Pty.) Ltd., 24 Sturdee Avenue, Rosebank, Johannesburg 2196, South Africa

Penguin Books Ltd., Registered Offices: 80 Strand, London WC2R 0RL, England

International Standard Book Number: 978-1-59257-749-1

Library of Congress Catalog Card Number: 2007932655

10 09 08   8 7 6 5 4 3 2 1

Interpretation of the printing code: The rightmost number of the first series of numbers is the year of the book's printing; the rightmost number of the second series of numbers is the number of the book's printing. For example, a printing code of 08-1 shows that the first printing occurred in 2008.

Printed in the United States of America

Note: This publication contains the opinions and ideas of its authors. It is intended to provide helpful and informative material on the subject matter covered. It is sold with the understanding that the authors and publisher are not engaged in rendering professional services in the book. If the reader requires personal assistance or advice, a competent professional should be consulted.

The authors and publisher specifically disclaim any responsibility for any liability, loss, or risk, personal or otherwise, which is incurred as a consequence, directly or indirectly, of the use and application of any of the contents of this book.

Most Alpha books are available at special quantity discounts for bulk purchases for sales promotions, premiums, fund-raising, or educational use. Special books, or book excerpts, can also be created to fit specific needs.

For details, write: Special Markets, Alpha Books, 375 Hudson Street, New York, NY 10014.

Publisher: *Marie Butler-Knight*

Editorial Director: *Mike Sanders*

Managing Editor: *Billy Fields*

Acquisitions Editor: *Michele Wells*

Development Editor: *Ginny Bess Munroe*

Senior Production Editor: *Jan Lynn*

Copy Editor: *Ginny Bess Munroe*

Cover/Book Designer: *Kurt Owens*

Indexer: *Heather McNeill*

Layout: *Ayanna Lacey*

Proofreader: *Aaron Black*

Contents at a Glance

Contents

Appendixes

Introduction

You've probably heard more than you wanted to know about Webkinz® animals and how fabulous they are from your child, but if you've wandered online to check out the online component—Webkinz World—you may very well have been overwhelmed. The site is huge!

In addition to interacting with the online version of their plush pets, children who enter Webkinz World have literally hundreds of things they can do while there. From playing games to completing educational quizzes, creating animated movies, caring for their virtual pet, earning cash to fund their online play, chatting and hanging out anonymously with other pet owners, and decorating a special home for their Webkinz animal, Webkinz World offers a wealth of online activities.

Things to Help You Out Along the Way

You will notice throughout the chapters some special messages along the way.

Keep It Simple
Facts and figures about Webkinz World.

def•i•ni•tion
These notes clarify terminology.

Tip
Lesser-known tactics for succeeding at particular games.

Warning
Cautionary notes to help you stay out of trouble and avoid disappointment.

According to Grant
Tips from a seven-year-old Webkinz guru to help you get the most out of Webkinz World.

Acknowledgments

Our deep gratitude goes to our experienced group of Webkinz owners, who offered many tips and strategies for getting the most out of Webkinz World. These friends, relatives, and classmates include Connor Severino of Massachusetts; Bennett Turner, Chandler Turner, and Cheryl Turner of New Jersey; Libby Kellmanson of New York; Morgan Ingalls of New York; and, of course, Amanda and Charlie Turner, our biggest cheerleaders.

We'd also like to thank our always-helpful agent Marilyn Allen of the Allen O'Shea Literary Agency, our terrific editor Michele Wells, technical editor Cheryl Bavaro, and the whole Alpha team for their support.

Trademarks

All terms mentioned in this book that are known to be or are suspected of being trademarks or service marks have been appropriately capitalized. Alpha Books and Penguin Group (USA) Inc. cannot attest to the accuracy of this information. Use of a term in this book should not be regarded as affecting the validity of any trademark or service mark.

Webkinz, Webkinz World, Kinzcash, W Shop, W, Webkinz Newz, Quizzy's Question Corner, Kinzchat, Lil' Kinz, and all character names and game names are trademarks owned by the GANZ.

Chapter 1

Getting Started

In This Chapter

- ◆ Adopting a Webkinz®
- ◆ Choosing a unique name
- ◆ Keeping your pet alive
- ◆ Buying the online essentials

You did it! You are among the few, the proud, who managed to find a Webkinz animal in stock somewhere. With the popularity of Webkinz rivaling, or even surpassing, that of Beanie Babies, getting to the point of entering the online Webkinz World is an accomplishment.

Of course, plush Webkinz are cuddly and entertaining on their own, even without using the attached computer code to venture onto the Internet to explore. Many young children are perfectly content to play for hours with their stuffed Webkinz and Lil' Kinz®.

For many elementary school-age children, ages 6 to 13, Webkinz World is where all the fun is. It's where children can play computer games, enter contests, challenge friends to games, and buy paraphernalia to give to their beloved animals.

What Are Webkinz?

Webkinz are plush pets that come equipped with a special computer code that gives the bearer access to Webkinz World. The pets come in two varieties: Webkinz and their smaller cousins Lil' Kinz. There are currently around 60 different Webkinz animals, which include several dog breeds, horses, frogs, cats, bears, and even a mythical Pegasus. Lil' Kinz are available in about 30 varieties that match Webkinz; however, they are about two-thirds the size, hence the name. Webkinz currently cost around $13 and Lil' Kinz cost around $10. Both provide one year of access to Webkinz World.

Tip

How do you know if you have a Webkinz? Check the bottom of the animal's paws for a multicolored "W." The latest animals have a W on them, but the absence of one might just mean you have an older model. Check the online Webkinz catalog to be sure.

Because there are so many different types of cute, stuffed animals on the market, Ganz, the maker of Webkinz, embroiders a "W" on its to help identify which are true Webkinz pets.

Types of Activities

With so many new websites developed for children to play in, Webkinz World is one of the real bargains. Other sites often charge a monthly fee for access, whereas this one is included free in the price of the cute, stuffed pet.

Inside Webkinz World, children can study facts and figures, play Arcade games, learn about money management, decorate rooms for their pets, visit with other kids in a safe online clubhouse, and send notes to each other using a restrictive dictionary. That is, there is a selection of words and phrases Webkinz owners can use to communicate with each other, but some words are forbidden, such as inappropriate terms, expletives, or anything that might give personal details, such as any kind of number.

To enjoy the fun and games inside Webkinz world, owners have to log in at the Webkinz home page.

Skills Developed

By spending time in Webkinz World, children become more familiar with the proper use of a computer, strengthen their keyboarding skills, work on spelling and word formations, improve memory skills, and have fun. The site is certainly focused on having fun, but many of the activities are at least partially educational.

Related Products

Although Webkinz pets have been around since 2005, it wasn't until 2007 that the cuties really took off. Now, faced with seeming unending demand for the pets, Ganz, the company that developed Webkinz, is in the process of rolling out related products. Webkinz Trading Cards have already been introduced, in addition to plush carrying cases for the animals. Word is that charms are also on their way.

The Adoption

With the purchase of a Webkinz animal or Lil' Kinz, you are entitled to one year of access to Webkinz World. This online website, at www.webkinz.com, is where your child can interact with her pet, which has a virtual alter ego that looks like a cartoon version of the stuffed animal.

However, before your child can explore the fun and games online, she first needs to officially adopt a Webkinz. Essentially, children register a pet with the online system.

Creating an Account

After you bring up the home page at www.webkinz.com, in the center of the screen, click on the "New Member" icon under the words "Log In."

You meet Ms. Birdy, an animated goose who processes all Webkinz adoptions. If this is your first Webkinz, Ms. Birdy tells you that you need to register as a new user and set up a new account.

> **Keep It Simple**
>
> If this is your child's second, third, or twelfth Webkinz pet, you'll want to click on the "Log into My Account" button at this stage, so that the new pet can be added to your child's existing account, rather than creating a new one. Setting up a new account for each animal can get confusing and make it more difficult to check on and care for them. Stick with one account for all your animals.

To set up a new account, you or your child need to read through the standard agreement and click "OK" if you agree to the terms.

On the next screen, your child is asked to provide his first name, date of birth, gender, and what country he lives in. If you live in the United States, you are also asked to indicate which state you live in.

After you click the word "Next" at the bottom right corner of the page, you are taken to a new screen where you are asked to choose a username. Your username should not be your real name, and it needs to be at least four characters. It should include letters and/or numbers.

Selecting a Username

With so many children already registered at Webkinz, it can get tricky to find a username that isn't already taken. Here are some ideas for coming up with a username your child can remember and that is available. Ask your child the following questions:

◆ What is your nickname?

◆ What is your favorite food?

◆ What is your favorite sport?

◆ What is your favorite animal?

◆ What are you good at?

◆ Add a number, such as your favorite sports star's jersey number, to your nickname or another word.

◆ Add your age to another word you select, either at the front or at the end of the word.

According to Grant

"I came up with my username by thinking about things I liked and things I was good at. For example, if you're good at basketball, you might choose a name using a word like 'net' or 'hoop.'"

Your child's username appears on the screen when he participates in any tournaments, such as playing checkers against a friend, so keep this in mind as he selects it. You don't want a phrase or username that embarrasses your child.

After you choose a username, click "Next" to learn whether it has been accepted. If someone else is already using the same username, you immediately see a note that says the username has already been selected, so please choose a different one. Then try again by adding a number or using a slightly different spelling.

Choosing a Password

Next, choose a secret password that is at least six letters and/or numbers. This is a combination of letters and numbers that you want your child to keep to himself so that no one else can log in and pretend to be him.

Keep your password as simple as possible, something you can easily remember. It can be a combination of numbers, such as a phone number or street address, or a word you like. You don't have to worry that someone else might be using the same password, so choose one that you won't forget. Then, click "Next."

Finally, your child needs to remove the little slip of paper enclosed in the clear plastic envelope attached to her Webkinz's paw. On the slip of paper is a unique alphanumeric code, which you need to enter on the screen to prove you purchased an official Webkinz. After typing in the code, place that little piece of paper somewhere safe, in case your computer crashes and you need to retype the information later. That code proves your child owns a Webkinz.

After entering the code, your child will be asked to type some letters shown on the screen. These letters simply verify that a real person is entering the information and not a computer program. Type them and then click "Next."

Your child's next task is naming her pet and determining whether it is a boy or girl.

Naming Your Webkinz

Your child has only one chance—and this is it—to name her new Webkinz, so be sure she likes the name.

Here are some questions to ask that might help you find the perfect name for your child's new pet:

- What color is the Webkinz?

- What kind of animal is it?

- From what part of the world does it come?

- Does the Webkinz have any distinguishing characteristics, such as soft fur or big ears?

- What are some names your child likes?

 Tip

Tons of websites help people name their pets, so why not use those same sites to pick the best name for your Webkinz? Some of the largest are www. bowwow.com.au, www. petnamesworld.com, and www.babynames.com/ Names/Pets.

After your child selects a name, types it into the form, and then decides whether it is a boy or girl, your child will receive an adoption certificate with the pet's birthday and personality description. You can even print out the information.

The next page you see is a summary of all the information your child has just entered. Put this information in a safe place, in case your child forgets his or her username or password. You can also print this page.

After all the paperwork is done, you can either watch a quick onscreen demo with your child, which shows you how to set up your pet's online room and the basics of how Webkinz World works, or your child can go right to playing games and having fun.

Webkinz World

Ah, the wonderful world of Webkinz. There are so many fun activities that it's hard to know where to start. So let's start with your child's pet.

How Is Your Pet Doing?

On the bottom left of the first screen you see when you log into the Webkinz website is a little picture of your pet and its health, happiness, and hunger levels. The goal is to keep your Webkinz as close to possible to 100 percent happy, healthy, and fed. That's not hard with a little bit of attention every few days.

To make sure your pet is happy, healthy, and well-fed, keep an eye on the health, happiness, and hunger meter in the bottom left of the Webkinz World screen.

Your child's Webkinz is nearly always happy, but visiting the pet from time to time, by choosing "My Room" from the Things to Do menu bar on the bottom-right, is sure to keep a smile on the pet's little face. It's a pop-up bar, so click "Things to Do" and a list of available activities displays. On the list is My Room. Choose this option to go to your pet's room for a visit.

You can access all the activities in Webkinz World through the Things to Do menu, which is in the bottom right and pops up on the screen when you click on it.

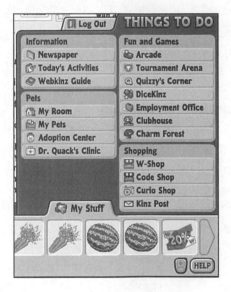

Is Your Pet Ill?

Webkinz pets are generally healthy, but too much activity or junk food can make them sick.

The first thing to do if you or your child sees that the Webkinz is feeling under the weather is to head to Dr. Quack's Clinic, which is found under the Things to Do menu bar. A click on the Dr. Quack's Clinic button immediately delivers your child's Webkinz to the doctor, who examines the pet behind a curtain and makes a diagnosis. A frequent diagnosis is too little sleep or a poor diet.

Although Webkinz never die, they do get sick if you don't feed them or spend any time with them. Children will know their pets are ill when they see the blue ice pack on their heads and thermometer in their mouths.

To treat your child's Webkinz, suggest that your child buy healthier food for it from the W Shop, which can be found under the Things to Do menu bar. Although there is a huge variety of munchies under the food category at the W Shop, sticking with fruits and vegetables helps avoid future visits to Dr. Quack.

The good news is that there is a limit to how sick a Webkinz can get, and although a Webkinz account is considered inactive after 90 days, Webkinz do not die.

Tip

If your child takes his Webkinz to Dr. Quack's Clinic, he is likely to hear the doctor tell him that his pet needs more sleep. The best way to ensure a good night's rest is to move the Webkinz into its bed before leaving Webkinz World each day. You can buy a bed at the W Shop and place it in My Room.

Is That a Stomach Rumbling?

Like most animals, Webkinz get hungry and need food. You'll know how hungry your child's Webkinz is by looking at its hunger level in the lower-left corner of the screen. The lower the number falls—with 1 being ravenous and 100 being well-fed—the more food your child needs to purchase and feed the pet.

To purchase food, click on the "Things to Do" menu bar, and then click "W Shop," where you can find virtually everything your child needs to care for his Webkinz. One of the categories of products available for purchase with *KinzCash®* is food. Click Food, and you see boxes of pictures of food with the associated prices.

Under each picture of the different types of food is the cost in KinzCash. Most food, such as blueberries, apples, and water, costs 5 KinzCash. As you click food to purchase, which you do by clicking "Add to Cart," you see how much you've spent so far at the bottom of the screen, along with how much KinzCash you have left to spend.

After you make your selections—and you can choose as many of each as you can afford—click "Check Out." The total cost is immediately deducted from your KinzCash stash, and the food moves into your *dock* at the bottom of the screen.

> **Keep It Simple**
>
> Some types of food are specially formulated for your child's type of Webkinz, such as the Frozen Iceberg Chili for polar bears and Bueno Bone Burritos for Chihuahuas. Keep an eye out in the W Shop for food your pet will particularly enjoy.

def•i•ni•tion

KinzCash is the Webkinz World equivalent of money. Your child is given 2,000 KinzCash to start and can earn more through a variety of fun and educational activities. Remember, those 2,000 KinzCash bucks can be quickly spent on pet necessities.

Your **dock** is where all your purchases are stored after your child buys them from the W Shop or Curio Shop. The dock is essentially a closet and refrigerator in one. To move items from your dock into the Webkinz room, place your cursor on them, one at a time and drag them into the room.

You can easily keep track of what you've already purchased or won by looking at your dock at the bottom of your screen. Your dock is essentially your storage area for goodies.

To feed your child's Webkinz, put your cursor on the food in your dock and drag it onto the pet. You can do this when the animal is in its room—My Room—or by dragging the food left onto the little picture of the pet on the main screen. The food must be "fed" to the pet by being moved on top of it rather than simply placing it into its room or near it.

According to Grant

"When my Webkinz's hunger level gets in the 50s, I just go to the W Shop and buy healthy food such as blueberries and broccoli."

Decorating My Room

In addition to feeding the pet and visiting, you'll want to buy your child's Webkinz a bed and some play things. These pieces of furniture and accessories go into its room, which you enter by clicking "Things to Do" to bring up the menu and then clicking "My Room."

Although every newly-registered Webkinz comes with 2,000 KinzCash, the Webkinz's room is totally bare. When you click "My Room" and make your first visit, you see two walls and a floor that are gray. No windows, no furniture, and no color can be seen. These things can certainly be purchased with those 2,000 virtual bucks.

Tip

Your child might be eager to spiff up her pet's online room, but to avoid a mishmash of styles and colors, you might want to suggest a look at the variety of theme rooms Webkinz has created. Going with a theme, such as cheerleading or baseball, for example, can help your child choose coordinating furniture, paint colors, and accessories. Click "Room Themes" in the W Shop, and you'll see the options.

There is no requirement that your child purchase anything, of course, but because every Webkinz needs its rest, it might be a good idea to at least buy a bed.

Home Furnishing 101

Other types of furniture your child can buy include chairs, tables, appliances, decorations, windows, flooring, and paint for the wall, to name just a few accoutrements.

Some of the extras work only in outdoor rooms, which can be purchased for 1,000 KinzCash and added to the one room you started with. Some children build extensive homes with rooms of every type and theme, including a backyard and front yard. But accessories such as hammocks can be placed only in an outdoor area, so don't buy those types of items until you have an outdoor room.

Pet Activities

Because your child will certainly not want his Webkinz to grow bored when he's at school and cannot play, buying some games for the pet to entertain himself is a popular choice. What's exciting about the games, however, is that they are interactive and can be played against an opponent just like the games in the Tournament Arena. Where the Arcade has one-person games, the Tournament Arena has games for two or more competitors.

For example, Dogbeard's Bathtub Battles, which is available at the W Shop for 350 KinzCash, is a cool, interactive game of battleship that pits your child's Webkinz pet against a virtual opponent for a KinzCash prize. Inside the room is a wooden bathtub with ships floating in it. When you click it, your child's Webkinz walks over to it, and a new screen opens so that the game can be played.

> **Tip** _____
>
> Before your child purchases a game for his pet, double-check that it is interactive and not just decorative. Games that are interactive have a bright blue semicircle in the bottom right of the description in the W Shop that reads "Interactive." Those that are for show only do not have the blue indicator.

Some other fun interactive games you can purchase for your child's pet include the card game Go Fish, checkers, air hockey—Grant's personal favorite—a jigsaw puzzle, and Farming Frenzy, to name a few.

Each game has impressive graphics that make even Rock, Paper, Scissors—the simplest of games—fun.

Of course, there are also toys and books available, such as a baseball mitt and ball, a bowling ball and set of pins, a silly looking clown doll, or a set of three crayons. And the books, such as *Does the Caged Singoz Sing?*, contain real stories that can be read and reread.

If your child's preferences, or the Webkinz's tastes, change, it is easy to sell any purchases back to the W Shop. Click "Things to Do" and then click "W Shop," and in the bottom-right corner, you see a button labeled "Sell." To sell something the Webkinz has outgrown, move it from the dock into the W Shop, where you will be given a price the shop is willing to pay for the item.

If your child suddenly decides that her frog would rather spend time in an outdoor-themed space than a jungle-themed room, or his horse would prefer a sports-themed room, it's easy to clear out the old and purchase the new. However, because the W Shop does not issue credit, your child needs to have enough KinzCash in his account before attempting to buy something.

You can quickly see how much KinzCash you have by looking to the right of the picture of your Webkinz, down in the lower-left corner of your computer screen. The number following the "W" with whiskers is your total KinzCash.

> **Warning** _____
>
> Although it is certainly easy to sell back items your child has purchased for his Webkinz, be aware that the money earned generally is 50 percent of the original cost. So, you might want to suggest that your child be sure about that trendy pop star bed before plunking down 950 KinzCash for it.

In addition to spending KinzCash on furnishings and food, you might want to encourage your child to bank those KinzCash to buy and furnish other rooms, or to do fun things such as make movies, which require KinzCash to produce.

The Least You Need to Know

◆ Webkinz stuffed animals are fun to play with on their own, without the online element.

◆ Choosing a username for your child and a name for the Webkinz doesn't have to be difficult. Turn to pet naming websites for inspiration.

◆ You can closely monitor the happiness, health, and hunger of your child's Webkinz from the first screen, along with how much KinzCash is available to spend.

◆ To keep your child's animal healthy, be sure to place it in bed everyday after your child is done playing and feed it plenty of fruits, vegetables, and water. Don't worry though—Webkinz never die.

◆ Your child receives 2,000 KinzCash for the first animal she registers (additional Webkinz come with increasing amounts of KinzCash).

Chapter 2

Earning Cash ... and What You Can Buy

In This Chapter

- ◆ Quick ways to earn KinzCash®
- ◆ Daily to-do's
- ◆ Spending opportunities
- ◆ Selling stuff back

At the heart of the appeal of Webkinz® is a child's ability to take full responsibility for and control of caring for his virtual pet. Kids are the sole provider for their animal(s)—buying food, clothing, and shelter, as well as fun interactive games and toys, of course. For school-age kids, this experience can be empowering and rewarding, even if we *are* talking about a computer-generated image.

What parents might appreciate is that their children must manage their money well within Webkinz World to afford purchases. And children quickly learn that things cost money, even in a virtual world. Everything from a new outdoor play area to cool sunglasses to a bottle of water for their pet requires them to spend their hard-earned online bucks. This chapter looks at how children can earn KinzCash.

Ways to Earn KinzCash

Fortunately, there are several daily opportunities kids can take advantage of to earn some quick cash.

Daily Activities

One of the best places to start is in the Today's Activities tab listed in the Things to Do menu bar. There, you find daily opportunities to get some free KinzCash, as well as hourly deals and offers. Sometimes, those deals are for a percent-off coupon at the W Shop; other times, the hourly offer might be for an extra spin on the Wheel of Wow. Scope out the day's special deals to be sure you don't miss out.

Wheel of Wow

One of the easiest ways to earn some free KinzCash is by taking a daily spin of the Wheel of Wow. Each of the 10 pie-shaped spaces on the wheel offers Webkinz owners the chance for a little KinzCash or a special prize, which might be even more KinzCash or a treat for your child's pet.

Simply click "Spin" to get the wheel in motion, and when it stops automatically a few turns later, you find out what you won that day.

Any KinzCash you earn is automatically deposited in your account and immediately available to spend. Of course, you could also get a bucket of Gak, which might be a meal but looks disgusting.

Wishing Well

Also found under Today's Activities, The Wishing Well 2 game, which is a bird's eye view of a water well, gives you five chances daily to rack up some cash by matching shapes. There is no skill involved, just click on "Play," and then "Make a Wish."

Simply click on "Spin" and you can earn a free treat—anything from KinzCash to clothes, furniture, or food.

Click on "Make a Wish" and you can earn up to 3,000 KinzCash just by looking into the well.

According to Grant

"The most you can get at the Wishing Well is 3,000 KinzCash. The most I've ever gotten is 1,000, though, if you get three wishing wells lined up in the center."

The amount you win varies according to the particular combination of fruit, animal heads, wishing well, or W icons that appear in any of the three lines. If you succeed in getting any of those combinations in the middle row, rather than the top or bottom, you receive three times the normal amount of KinzCash.

There is no strategy for getting a better spin, just luck. But in less than a minute, you can collect a bunch of free KinzCash at The Wishing Well 2.

Daily KinzCare

Another easy activity that can net your child a little KinzCash and a tasty treat for her Webkinz is found in Daily KinzCare, which is in the My Pets section of the site. It takes only a minute or two to do and is certainly worth a couple of mouse clicks.

Click "Things to Do" to bring up the menu and then click on "My Pets" at the bottom of the list.

By clicking on the current day of the week in KinzCare, you can earn a little cash and a food treat.

A screen pops up that summarizes your Webkinz's status—happiness, health, and hunger—on the first page. Then, if you click the tab at the top that reads "Daily KinzCare," you see another page with seven boxes at the top—one for each day of the week. Every day you click on the phrase "I love my Webkinz!," your child earns a Care Award that consists of a food treat for his pet, such as an omelet or spaghetti and some KinzCash.

This is one of the lesser-known ways to earn some quick cash.

> **According to Grant**
>
> "If you visit the Daily KinzCare section every day for a week, you might win a prize. Not everyone remembers to go there every day."

Gem Hunt

One of the most exciting daily activities is Arte's Gem Hunt, which is located within the Curio Shop. To get there, click on "Things to Do" and then "Curio Shop." A new computer screen opens with a talking dog named Arte who explains the Curio Shop, which sells unique Webkinz items. More importantly for kids interested in earning KinzCash, Arte also buys gems from children who go hunting for them. Everyone has one chance a day to go on a gem hunt within one of the five mines.

After listening to Arte's introduction, click the "Gem Hunt" button in the bottom-right corner of the screen. You'll be taken to another screen showing the mines to search: Barking Mad Mine, Buried Bones Mine, Flea Floater Mine, Howling Horse Mine, and Muzzle Mouth Mine. Click any of the mines—there's no way to know which one is going to have the best gems—and you are brought into a chamber within the mine.

You can move to the left or the right in search of little nuggets that might or might not be gems—use your cursor and point at the left or right directional buttons to get your little mining car with flashlight to move.

> **Tip**
>
> Some Webkinz owners claim that moving to the left or the right of the first screen, instead of choosing one of the rocks right in front of them, improves their odds of finding gems.

For a hint about where to look for different colored gems, check out Appendix C.

Then use your pick axe to tap on any of the little ovals—which are possible gems—above or below the opening. You have three chances to find a gem, and as soon as you do, your turn is over. However, there is plenty of slag in the mines as well, and you might go several days without finding anything of value.

Arte has a "Gem of the Day," which can yield a pretty penny if you happen to find it. But there are a total of 30 gems out there to be found.

After you find a gem, a new screen pops up in which Arte congratulates you for finding a particular gem. He also makes you an offer in KinzCash, in case you're interested in selling. If it's rare, Arte might offer several hundred in KinzCash, and if it's pretty common, as little as 20 KinzCash.

According to Grant

"I usually sell my gems to get more KinzCash. I sold one gem for more than 300. It's pretty easy to find gems, and sometimes I need KinzCash right away so that I can buy something else."

Keep in mind that although the cash is enticing, you might want to hold onto the gems you find and try to complete the Crown of Wonder, which consists of 30 different gems.

The Crown of Wonder is like a trophy you can wear to show everyone you found all 30 gems. After you have filled in Your Gem Box with five gems in each color—white, yellow, blue, green, and red—you can click the crown icon on Your Gem Box, and Arte makes a Crown of Wonder for you.

There is no limit to the number of Crowns of Wonder you can earn, and they are worth 2,500 KinzCash.

Employment Office

Another daily activity that generates KinzCash is the Employment Office, which offers several different jobs where Webkinz owners can work: for example, Dr. Quack's Assistant, Fence Painting, Hamburger Cook, Piano Player, Flooring Assistant, Newz Delivery, Gem Mining, and Shoe Store Clerk, to name a few. You can actually work at a job once every eight hours, and the jobs available to you change each time you visit.

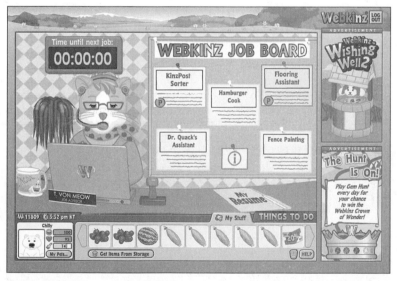

Every eight hours you can head to the Employment Office to put in some time at one of several jobs available where you can earn some KinzCash.

Although each job is different, they all require a variation of matching skills. You can learn more about the specifics of each job in Chapter 4.

Each time your child performs the job satisfactorily, making the right matches in the allotted time, she receives payment starting at 50 KinzCash. If she can't complete the task in the time given, she does not

According to Grant

"My favorite job is Dr. Quack's Assistant because it's a little harder than the other jobs. You have to give the animals the right medicine to make them feel better."

get paid. The summary resumé that pops up after each attempt breaks down how many times each job has been attempted, what level your child is working at, and what the pay rate for each job is. It is essentially a tally of all the different jobs your child has attempted and how well they've done.

Keep It Simple

After your child successfully completes the same job in the Employment Office three times, he earns a raise—more KinzCash—the next time he completes the same task.

Weekly Survey in the *Newz*

Completing a survey that is announced in the Newspaper is another way to earn some quick KinzCash once a week. It's a little tough to find, however.

Weekly one-question surveys in the Webkinz Newspaper can net your child 50 KinzCash.

Click the "Newspaper" listing in the Things to Do menu. Then click "Contact Us" in the bottom right corner of the page. On the next screen, click the tab at the top that reads "Comments and Suggestions." On the right side of that page is a weekly survey that gives you 50 KinzCash for answering.

This week's survey was about which of five room themes should be retired soon. As soon as you make your selection, 50 KinzCash is deposited in your account.

Game of the Day

Everyday Webkinz announces a Game of the Day on the Arcade page, on the right-hand side. The Game of the Day gives out bonus KinzCash just for playing. When you finish playing the game, you receive a total for the amount of KinzCash you won and the total bonus you received.

The game changes daily, so be sure and read Today's Activities to know which Arcade game to try. In addition to boosting your KinzCash account, you get the chance to try a bunch of new games.

Quizzes, Games, and Tournaments

In addition to daily and weekly activities that give away free cash, there are also unlimited ways your child can earn more money.

Quizzes

In addition to the daily activities that generate KinzCash, children can also earn virtual money by taking quizzes testing their knowledge of social studies, math, the arts, health, language, and science by going to Quizzy's. Just head to Things to Do and click the "Quizzy's" button.

Tip

Within Quizzy's, you can find a Bonus Question on the left side of the page that gives you 8 KinzCash for a correct answer, which you can do once a day. Regular Quizzy's answers pay 5 KinzCash.

> **Warning** _____
>
> To qualify for the Piano Player job in the Employment Office, you need to have completed a set of 50 Quizzy's questions. You can't take the job until you complete the specified 50 questions.

When in the Quizzy's area, click the age range appropriate for your child. You can choose from 5 to 6, 7 to 8, 9 to 10, 11 to 12, 13+, and Everyone. The questions grow harder, the older the age range. For example, a 5-to-6-year-old math question might require adding 3 and 2, whereas one for 13+ year olds might ask the definition of the word "mean" or what the "nth" number is.

Games

Your child also earns KinzCash for every game he plays within the Arcade, which is found on the Things to Do menu bar on the right.

We'll go into the specifics of playing the 20+ Webkinz games in Chapter 3, but the general idea is that kids can choose from a long list of challenges. Some are one-person games and some are two-person.

Some games require the use of the arrow keys on the keyboard to navigate and others rely on the cursor. Most are just plain fun, but there are also motor skills being developed and keyboard familiarization in some of the games.

The amount of KinzCash earned from playing each game depends on how far your child gets. That is, some games pay out 1 KinzCash for every 350 points, for example, whereas others pay out at every 500 points. And if a child didn't earn the minimum number of points required, there is no KinzCash pay out.

Tournaments

Games in which you compete against other Webkinz owners are called tournaments and are found in the Tournament Arena within Things to Do.

As a competitor in a tournament, you can either play against another Webkinz owner or against several players. When you click on the name of the game in the Tournament Arena that you want to play, a new window will pop up that links you with another player. You don't know anything about him or her besides his or her Webkinz's name, but the two of you try and best the other.

Some tournaments allow you to compete against several other players during the course of a day, potentially winning the prize and a trophy for the best score. This is the case in one-person games such as Cash Cow or Candy Bash, for example, which are not set up to be two-person games.

Tournaments allow you to earn a little more KinzCash if you win, but even if you lose, you still get a small cash prize for playing.

Sell Items You Previously Bought

Another way to earn KinzCash is to sell back items you previously bought at the Curio Shop or W Shop. However, because your child will likely receive only 50 percent of the original price she paid in exchange for selling off her prior purchases, reselling is not the greatest financial move. Then again, some rooms are so overloaded with stuff that clearing them out and making some quick cash doesn't sound like such a bad idea. (You do know we're talking about the Webkinz rooms, right?)

If you get tired of items you've purchased at the W Shop, it's quick and easy to sell them back to recoup some KinzCash, but you'll only get 50 percent of the original price.

The selling process is quite simple, too. Start by heading to the W Shop, accessible through the Things to Do menu bar on the right. On the first screen that pops up, listing all the categories of products available at the W Shop, you see a Sell button on the bottom right. Click that to start.

A new window pops up with empty squares in the upper–left corner. Those are storage units, essentially, into which you need to move any items you want to sell. Just drag them from your dock up to one of the squares.

A message appears that tells you how much you can make from selling each particular item. And you can decide whether to keep each or sell them based on that quote. If you want to sell, just click Sell, and immediately your account will be credited. And if you decide you'd rather keep an item, just move it back into your dock. If you have several items you want to sell at once, be sure and move any items back into your dock that you decide to keep before clicking Sell—anything in those boxes will be sold as soon as you click.

Tip

Even food you received as freebies can be sold back. That unappealing orange Gak, for example, is worth 3 KinzCash, believe it or not. Click "Sell"!

Selling cast-offs, even if they are virtual-playing games, completing quizzes, and taking advantage of the daily freebies, can quickly help you line your KinzCash account. But then what? What can your child *do* with all the cash? Believe us, there are plenty of spending opportunities in Webkinz World!

What You Can Buy

The entire point of earning KinzCash, in addition to bragging rights, is to afford the essentials—food, clothing, and shelter. What? You're not convinced your child's virtual pet needs cowboy boots or sunglasses? Well, okay, clothing isn't really an essential in Webkinz World, but it sure is fun!

In addition to clothing, you can use KinzCash to stock up on yummy food to keep your pet healthy, as well as home décor items to help it feel comfortable and loved.

Food and Drink for Your Pet

Webkinz animals don't need much to keep them happy, other than visits from their owner, but to stay healthy, they need a steady diet of healthy fruits and vegetables. Sure, you can also buy them fun food like cake, cookies, and soda, but too much junk food and they become ill.

To buy food, head to the W Shop, which is on the main Things to Do menu. When there, click the "Food" category, and you see minipictures of the many dishes you can buy your pet. Parents will notice that the healthier fare comes first, on the first page, but there are plenty of other offerings—some healthy, some not so much.

To view all the dishes and drinks available for purchase, click the "Next" button on the bottom right and the next page of products appears. Next to the image and description of each type of food is its price.

Warning

Don't be surprised if your child complains that he can't buy some of the dishes his friends feed their Webkinz. Some food items are available universally, such as water and broccoli, but others are developed for and available only to certain animals.

Now, because you know you need to feed your Webkinz on a regular basis, just as humans need to eat regularly, too, consider trying to stock up on good food deals when you see them announced.

When you see a special price on blueberries announced in Daily Events, go buy a bunch at the lower price. Or if you get a coupon for the W Shop, and you can't think of anything you need right now, use it to buy a more expensive treat for your pet. That way you can spend less KinzCash on food you know your pet is eventually going to eat. And unlike in the real world, even fresh fruits and veggies don't go bad.

To feed your animal, just drag the food from your dock and place it overtop of him in My Room, and you'll receive an appreciative comment back. You also see its hunger rating climb a little for each piece of food or drink you give your pet.

Tip

On your Webkinz bio sheet, which you received when your child first registered her pet, you were told what one food your Webkinz loves most. For example, Polar Bears often love marshmallows. You can double-check this little fact by looking in the bio of the My Pets page.

Outfits and Accessories

Even more fun than feeding your Webkinz is dressing it up in cute virtual outfits. In the W Shop, you can find an amazing array of clothing and accessories for your animal. You can buy individual pieces, such as shirts, sweaters, shoes, belts, hair bows—you name it!

As with food, simply click the item you think would look great on your Webkinz and then click "Preview," if the option is available, to see what the item looks like on. Or just click "Check Out," and the item appears in your dock while your KinzCash account has the cost of the clothing deducted automatically.

Tip

Check the W Shop frequently for what's in the Sale Items category. There's no rhyme or reason for what's marked down, and you might spot those cool shoes you wanted at a great price. Just keep checking back daily to see what's on sale.

You can put together daily outfits, special occasion outfits, or outfits that match what your child likes to wear most often.

To put on or take off the different pieces of clothing you've bought, go to My Room and click the "Dress Your Pet" icon in the top-right corner of the screen. Up pops a screen showing all your various wardrobe essentials. You can then click them with your cursor and either place them on your Webkinz or drag them off your pet and into one of the storage squares to use later. Yes, in Webkinz World, there's no such thing as throwing worn outfits on the floor for later.

Furniture and Decorative Items

We left the discussion of decorating your Webkinz's room for last because some kids have been known to become obsessed with furnishing their pet's abode. Obsessed.

And who wouldn't? You have blank walls, a blank floor, and thousands of KinzCash at the start to spend on fun colors and homey accessories. Of course, your pet would be just fine with a bare room, but because getting rest is good for everyone—including a Webkinz—investing in a bed will probably reduce the number of visits you have to make to the Clinic.

What style bed would be best? That sets off a series of decisions about a theme for the room, or colors, or little extras.

If your child is overwhelmed by all the possible choices, a good place to start is by perusing the room themes that Webkinz has already put together and that are available in the W Shop.

According to Grant

"I didn't pick a theme for my rooms; I just bought fun things I thought my Webkinz would like, like a TV, a treadmill, a chair, and a refrigerator, where he can store his food."

When you click "Room Themes," you see a bunch of mini images showing ballet shoes, a car tire, a cat, a unicorn, and many, many others. Then, when you click one of those icons, you see several pieces that match that particular theme, which you can buy individually. For example, there are almost always beds, wall decorations, bedside tables, chairs, lamps, and even a sink and toilet, too.

Or click "Theme Preview" and get a taste of what a room totally decorated in that particular theme would look like. Unless your child has a huge stash of KinzCash, it's unlikely she can purchase everything in the room at once, but she can work toward a totally decked out room over time.

Furniture and decorations also go on sale, so watch the Sale Items, as well as special deals at the Curio Shop, where one-of-a-kind items frequently show up.

And, of course, after you decorate one room perfectly, it's time to buy another room, and another, and another—and an outdoor area for your pet to play in, where there is a whole new set of furniture options to explore. Some items can be used only outdoors, actually, so watch the fine print on any purchases before you buy them.

The Least You Need to Know

- There are five things you can do once a day to quickly earn KinzCash—Wheel of Wow, Wishing Well, Daily KinzCare, and Gem Hunt. You can also work at the Employment Office every eight hours and take a survey once a week.

- Be sure and look at the Hourly Events, listed under Today's Activities, for special sales, coupons, and extra chances to earn KinzCash.

- The best activities for racking up substantial points fairly quickly are the quizzes in Quizzy's, which are worth 5 KinzCash for each right answer.

- Another way to generate some quick KinzCash is to sell back items you bought that you don't want or need. The W Shop typically pays 50 percent of the original retail value for products you want to ditch.

- After earning thousands of KinzCash, your child is probably wondering what to do with it all. Some of the most common purchases are new rooms, accessories, and movie characters.

Chapter 3

Fun and Games

In This Chapter

- Playing in your room(s)
- Watching your pet play
- Heading down to the Arcade
- Competing in a tournament

The great thing about Webkinz® World is the variety of activities children have available to them. They can spend time in their pet's room playing games or watching their pet play, or they can head to the Arcade and test their skills at the 34 different games in the Arcade, or challenge opponents to a little one-on-one game play.

In this chapter, you learn how to play the many games and tournaments available in Webkinz World.

Hanging Out in Your Room

Just like at home, sometimes it's nice to hang out in your room. Except in this case, the room is in cyberspace, and it actually belongs to your Webkinz. It's still nice to get away, though.

In addition to surveying your space, you can do a number of things in your room.

Decorate

First and foremost, as we covered in Chapter 2, your child can go wild decorating and furnishing the room to her heart's content, or until she runs out of KinzCash®, whichever comes first.

> **According to Grant**
>
> "Adding a room is easy, but it costs money. I have 12 rooms, so my Webkinz has lots of places to go and play."

To add a room, go to My Room and click "Map" in the upper-left corner. You see a square in the center of the screen that is a birds-eye view of the one room your child now owns. To add onto that space, click "Add Room."

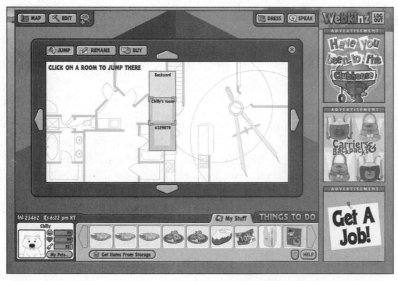

Buying additional rooms is easy, but you can never get rid of them, so be sure your Webkinz really needs the space before you spend your hard-earned KinzCash.

Four opaque squares appear around the existing room to show you where your next room can be placed. Select where you want the room to be—north, south, east, or west of the first room—and then select which kind of room you want. You're given a list of four types and the associated costs. They include the following:

◆ Large room 1,000

◆ Outdoor yard 1,000

◆ Medium room 700

◆ Small room 500

Click "Buy" next to the type of room you want, and you will be asked if you're sure that's what you want to do because adding a room can't be undone. When you click "yes," you are taken back to the Map in case you want to buy other rooms. When you finish adding rooms, close that window by clicking the small "x" in the upper–right corner.

Tip

You notice on the Map of your Webkinz's rooms that each one is labeled with a series of six numbers. You can easily change that so you know which is the bedroom, which is the dining room, and so on. Simply click the room you want to name, click "Rename" at the top of the page, and you see a field with the numbers in it. Highlight the numbers and type the room's name. Then, click "OK."

Play with Your Webkinz

Even with lots of rooms, your Webkinz can get bored just walking around. Fortunately, you can buy a bunch of fun toys for it to play on. Some of the cool items you can buy follow:

◆ Scooter

◆ Skateboard

◆ Swamp Runner fan boat

◆ Trampoline

◆ Treadmill

When your pet is on its toy, click where you want it to move, and it'll go there. For instance, when it's on its skateboard, you need to click in the room where you want the skateboard to roll to.

Your virtual Webkinz can ride on toys like scooters and skateboards in its room.

Play Games

In addition to helping your Webkinz have fun, you can play along using some of the interactive games, which we talked about in Chapter 1. These include the following:

- Air hockey
- Billiards
- Jigsaw puzzle
- Checkers
- Dogbeard's Bathtub Battles

- Farming Frenzy
- Go Fish card game
- Link'd
- Skunksweeper
- Zingoz Switcheroo

Keep It Simple _____

Many of the toys and games in the W Shop are for decoration only and cannot actually be played with, such as the basketball or bowling ball and bowling pins. They just sit in the room. If you want a toy that your pet can use, look for the "Interactive" symbol on the toy's picture when you click it.

To play, buy the game and move it from your dock to your room. Then, click it so that your pet will go over to play. The game should then load and display on your screen so you can begin.

Cook

When your pet gets hungry from all that activity, you might want to cook up a treat using some of the Webkinz appliances. Although many of the furnishings are for decoration only, some kitchen tools are interactive, just like the games. These include the following:

◆ Stoves

◆ Beach hibachi

◆ Cauldron

◆ Blenders

◆ Sandwich makers

◆ Grills

Designed to fit perfectly with your child's chosen room themes, these appliances can mix up tasty dishes using ingredients and cookbooks purchased at the W Shop.

Warning _____

Your child can literally spend hours and hours on Webkinz everyday, so you might want to set a limit on how much time he spends there. Yes, it has educational elements, but most of the games are pure fun.

Clean Your Pet

Of course, after a long day of playing and taste-testing, it might be a smart idea to clean your pet. Most Webkinz love the chance to take a long, hot bath, and you can find a wide variety of tubs for your Webkinz to soak in at the W Shop. Just look at the many types of tubs available:

◆ Clawfoot bathtub

◆ Football tub

◆ Funky girl bathtub

◆ High-tech bathtub

◆ Pirate's Rub-a-Dub Washtub

◆ Porcelain bathtub

◆ Sea blue bathtub

◆ Tin bucket tub

Some of the furniture you can buy is also interactive, such as the bathtub, where your pet can get clean.

After you move your tub into one of your rooms, have your animal get in the tub by clicking on it. You see a screen with your pet in the bath. You can use a sponge and soap or shampoo to scrub your pet clean, and it can play with a yellow rubber ducky while you work. When you finish cleaning it, click "All Done," and it'll towel off and get out, bringing you back to the room where the tub is located.

Tip

After you give your pet a bath, you can see its health meter increase because cleanliness is part of being healthy.

Invite Friends Over

Another fun thing to do in Webkinz World is to invite your child's friends—people on his Webkinz friends list—over to visit in his Webkinz's room. We talk about how to do this in Chapter 5, but we want to let you know this is another fun activity.

Tip

Webkinz holds fun contests involving room designs, writing, recipe design, and even TV show creation. You can earn KinzCash and maybe a trophy. Watch the Newspaper, listed in Things to Do, to find out when the next contest begins.

Arcade Games

Although you can find games in several places on Webkinz World, such as Today's Activities, the Arcade, which is listed in Things to Do, lists all the games. It's an excellent starting point to find your favorite. Note most games have a Show Me option, which gives a short demonstration regarding exactly how the game is played. It's a great way to quickly learn the ins and outs of a game you've never played before.

Ant Mania

Ant Mania involves moving your little black ant up and down a picnic blanket to gather food while avoiding little red ants and a big black spider.

You use your up and down arrow keys to move vertically and horizontally, but you can also hold two keys down and move diagonally, which can save time and get you out of trouble quickly. The longer you're on the picnic blanket, the more little red ants arrive on the scene, and eventually the big spider. If you come too close and they bite you, you're dead and the game is over. For every 15 points you earn, you get 1 dollar in KinzCash.

Tip

There are three special items you want to gather, in addition to the food. A sneaker makes you move faster, a snail makes the other ants and spider slow down, and a ladybug gives you a special shield that keeps you alive if you get bitten by one of the bad guys. Each lasts only a short time, however.

Bananza

In Bananza, you're a cute, little monkey walking along branches trying to gather yellow bananas to eat while avoiding the red spiders. Use the arrow keys to move sideways and the up arrow to jump.

Candy Bash

If you've ever seen Pong, an old Atari game, you'll get an idea of how to succeed at Candy Bash. The idea of the game is to help Poncho, who looks like a little Chihuahua, retrieve his candy from the piñata above. He uses a Mexican jumping bean that shoots out of his sombrero to knock the candy down. Your job is to keep the bean bouncing off his sombrero and to collect the candy and treats that fall down.

> **Tip**
>
> If you can catch multiple treats at once, you earn bonus points. Two pairs or three-of-a-kind earns you an extra 50 points, four of any combination gives you 100 points, and four-of-a-kind earns you an extra 200 points.

You can either use the left and right arrows to move Poncho back and forth under the candy or use your mouse—whichever is easier for you.

In addition to knocking down candy, the bean also knocks down toy rockets, which, if caught, shoot back up and knock down more candy for you to catch. Or it can unleash other beans, which can bounce and knock down candy.

You earn 1 KinzCash for every 125 points, and you get a trophy if you make it through all 30 levels of the game.

Candy Bash 2

Candy Bash 2 actually seems much easier than Candy Bash, because here you guide Poncho under the falling candy and use the Spacebar to shoot his bean up to break open the packages. After the package opens, the candy falls easily into his hat. Just don't move him too quickly.

The packages fall two or three at a time, giving you ample time at first to break open each one. When you get to the next level, it gets harder, of course, but at the start, it's quite manageable. In addition to using your mouse to move Poncho left and right under the falling candy, you can also use the arrow keys, along with the Spacebar.

It's important to catch the candy from each piñata, however, because if you miss three—or they land on Poncho's head—the game will be over. If the bean hits more than one piñata at a time, you can get extra points.

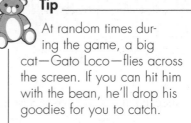

Tip

At random times during the game, a big cat—Gato Loco—flies across the screen. If you can hit him with the bean, he'll drop his goodies for you to catch.

Cash Cow

You can choose to play the easy or the hard version of Cash Cow, which is a fairly simple game to learn, though harder to master. The object is to click groups of three or more colored bottles to sell them, earning coins that get piled higher and higher in your waiting truck.

Keep the stacks of bottles low by removing as many colored groupings of bottles as possible. The groups need to be in a row of three or more or an L-shape with three or more in it. When you see a grouping, click it with your cursor, and the bottles are removed and sold with the rest consolidated, making other groups in the process.

As you remove bottles, the pile of money in the truck grows higher and higher, until you max out the capacity and go to the next level. Every 75 points you earn nets you 1 KinzCash dollar.

Each subsequent level of bottles starts with more layers to work through. And if the bottles bump up against the top of the screen, they crash and the game is over for you.

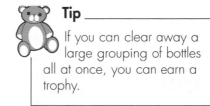

Tip

If you can clear away a large grouping of bottles all at once, you can earn a trophy.

Cash Cow 2

The board filled with color bottles is similar to the one you see in the original Cash Cow, but the game is played a little differently. In Cash Cow 2, the board starts full of colored bottles, and you try to remove them by clicking groups of two bottles of the same color. As you do, they are removed from the screen. Your goal is to clear the entire screen, earning points for each bottle you remove.

You find challenges along the way, namely some cracked bottles that break open and pour out, bottles with plus signs in them that add new bottles to the board, and a gray bottle that can't be removed except by cracking open a soda.

Some extra helpful bottles include gray ones with pop tops that explode and clear out all the bottles around them, including the gray ones with lids. The bottles with the lightning bolts clear all bottles with the same color cap as them and a yellow lightning bolt on a soda removes the entire row. The blue bottle with a lightning bolt on it clears all the bottles in the same row, and the bottles with "x2" on them are worth double points. If you can keep the dark gray square with the blue bottle on the screen, you also get extra points.

When you get to a point with no more groupings to remove, the level ends. But with 1 KinzCash for every 30 points, Cash Cow 2 is a little easier to earn money than with some other games.

Color Storm

Using the right and left arrow keys, the object of Color Storm is to match up four tiles—raindrops, essentially, of the same color, so they can fall from the sky. A cloud formation above drops colored drops into the sky, and you use the arrow keys to navigate the drops next to or below a tile of the same color.

Tip

Although you can't tell when the cloud will drop the colored rain onto the other tiles, you *can* tell which color it will be by looking at the under-side of the cloud. Before it drops a raindrop, the cloud pulsates a color, letting you know which color is coming next. Then you can plan where you want to move it before it falls.

Every few minutes a Rumble occurs where extra drops fall into the sky and cause other tiles to drop, creating new spots for colors to be placed.

Dashing Dolphin

Of all the games we tried, Dashing Dolphin seems to be among the hardest. The instructions are easy enough—swim through the water using the arrow keys to navigate and free friends in the nets as you go. The water current gives you extra speed, and if you jump through hoops, using the spacebar, you earn extra points.

You're timed, and if time runs out before you move through all the nets, the game is over.

What makes the game difficult is turning around if you miss a net or can't move quickly enough to follow the water current. You earn 1 KinzCash for every 80 points.

Dex Dangerous and the Lunar Lugbots

Dex Dangerous is a superhero working to protect the moon from Lugbotz who approach to mine it. If you've played Asteroids, this is similar. You use your mouse to move your spaceship on the screen, pressing the left mouse button to fire and destroy other ships that try to get onto the moon. They fly pretty quickly, so it's tricky to get all the way around the moon and shoot.

Special satellites, when shot, give Dex special powers. For every 40 points you earn, you get 1 KinzCash.

Go-Go Googles

One of the easier games (at least early on), Go-Go Googles involves moving Giggle and Gaggle (the Googles) to the left and right using your mouse. Click the mouse to throw the top Google up in the air to grab flowers—Gozies—and Buzzerflies. The object is to keep Buzzerflies from attaching to the Gozium Bramble in the middle of the screen. When five get attached, the bramble sneezes, and the game ends.

According to Grant

"I wait until I see a Buzzerfly coming, then I toss the Google in the air to try and stop the Buzzerfly from landing on the bramble."

If you click twice with your mouse, you can make the Googles flap, and if you tap the spacebar, you can switch which Google is on the top and which is on the bottom. The white Google can jump higher than the brown one, which can be useful if you try to nab high-flying Buzzerflies.

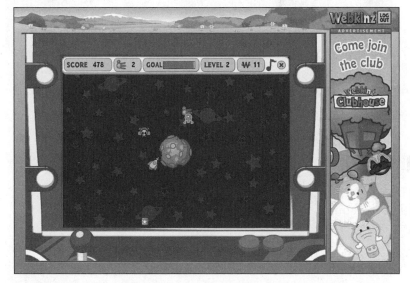

Dex Dangerous is very similar to Asteroids, the popular 1980s video game, and the object is to shoot other ships.

Goober's Lab

Goober's Lab is a lot like Bejeweled, another fun computer game you might have heard of. The object of the game is to line up three or more of the same colored atoms, which causes them to explode and the atoms above them to drop. You do this by swapping two adjacent atoms using your mouse to click the two atoms you want to move.

Each time you line up atoms to be exploded, you earn points, and you start to fill Goober's beaker. When it is full, you move to the next level. If you run out of time before the beaker is full, the game is over.

If you can spot lines or rows of three or more colored balls, you'll do well at Goober's Lab.

Hide n' Skunk

The object of Hide n' Skunk is to figure out where the skunks are hiding—you deduce where they are based on how many skunks are reported to be next to certain tiles.

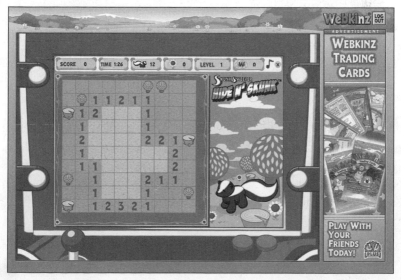

Hide n' Skunk is a game of deductive reasoning that will challenge even adults.

Based on the numbers telling you how many skunks are next to a tile, click tiles you think do *not* have skunks hiding under them. If you turn over a tile that does have a skunk, you earn a time penalty. Because you have only 1 minute 30 seconds total to uncover all the tiles except those where the skunks are, a time penalty can be costly. Many players simply run out of time before finding all the skunks.

Hungry Hog

If you enjoy the '80s video arcade game Ms. Pacman, you'll love Hungry Hog, which features a pig moving through a maze lined with junk food. The more junk food he eats, the more points he earns, but if he eats vegetables, which he hates, more junk food sprouts in the maze. The object of the game is to eat all the junk food without being stung by any bees, which are chasing him.

You use the arrow keys to navigate your way through the maze, which can be tricky. If you eat one of the little purple invincibility pills, you can eat the bees for a short period of time (around 20 seconds) while you swell up, but then your invincibility wears off, and your pig returns to its original size. If you get stung by a bee, you lose one of your lives—you start with three.

Tip

There is a passageway from one side of the maze to the other at the top and bottom of the screen that can help you quickly get away from a bee.

As you complete each level, you get a bonus and a new maze to work through. When you reach 5,000 points, you get an extra life.

Jazz Monsters

Jazz Monsters is a creative matching game. Five animals are playing jazz music, but monsters nearby hate the music and want to scare them away by flying down to spook them. When you see a monster, click the musician of the same color to get rid of the monster. The musician plays music and the monster pops.

If you don't move quickly enough, however, the monster scares the musician away, and you'll be left with fewer musicians. You can switch the remaining musicians around to play the needed instruments. Just click Switch, below the musician's instrument, and one of the other animals moves to play in his place.

You rack up points for each monster you get rid of, but after all the musicians have been scared away, the game is over.

Lily Padz

You'd think that making a frog jump from lily pad to lily pad would be easy, right? Well, it is and it isn't.

The game Lily Padz involves helping a frog jump home across lily pads of differing distances, using the arrow keys for direction and the spacebar to determine the trajectory of each longer jump. Pressing the left or right arrows makes the frog hop forward; the spacebar is for longer jumps over lots of water. The up arrow key also makes the frog jump into the air to catch yummy insects, although you want to steer clear of bees, which sting and cause the frog to lose power.

A power gauge is at the top of the screen that lets you know whether you have enough energy to make a big jump. If not, you need to replenish your energy by eating insects.

Every time you land in the water, you lose a try, and when you are out of tries, the game is over.

Lunch Letters

All the games in the Arcade are fun, but Lunch Letters helps build typing speed and accuracy by requiring your child to type the letters that appear on screen before they fall to the floor and get swept up by Billy the Goat, the school janitor. Proper keyboard positioning is also emphasized.

On Level One, mostly single letters fall and need to be typed, but by Level Three, two and three-letter words, such as "nay" and "jog" are more the norm, and more challenging to match quickly.

At the end of each level, you receive an assessment of your speed and accuracy, just as you would with a standard typing test.

Mini Golf

Anyone who loves playing miniature golf will surely get a kick out of Webkinz Mini Golf. To begin, you choose whether you want to play a one-person or two-person game. Then select which player you want to be from five different Webkinz characters—a basset hound, Labrador retriever, cat, or monkey. You then decide whether you want to play 18 holes or the front or back nine.

To begin, you move your mouse so that your player and the golf club are lined up with the hole. Then move the cursor away from your player to soften the shot or closer to make it stronger. Next, click the mouse, and your player swings. If you don't make it in the hole, your player moves up to meet the ball, and you line him up again with the hole and swing. It's easy to line the ball up properly, but nailing the right swing strength is tough.

Your score is tallied on a virtual golf score card, and KinzCash points are awarded based on how well you play.

Operation Gumball

To win Operation Gumball, you need to correctly guess a set of three numbers that shut down the gumball machine and prevent it from exploding (which it does if you run out of time).

You start by entering three numbers, such as 168 or 345. You get a gumball for each correct number—green for a number in the right position and red for a correct number in the wrong position. It's like the old game Mastermind, where you try and guess the four colored pegs your opponent has set up, using deductive reasoning.

With each try, you get more information about which numbers are or aren't in the code, and when you know all three numbers, you just need to figure out what order they should be in.

You can also play this as a two-person game, where the first person to correctly guess the code wins.

Picnic

Picnic is a faster version of Ant Mania, minus the red ants and spiders. The object of the game is to move your line of ants up and down the table cloth, which is like a grid, eating food along the way and avoiding falling off the edge. You use all the arrow keys—left, right, up, and down—to guide the first ant, working quickly to line the ant up with each morsel.

Each time you eat food, another ant joins the procession, and different food springs up elsewhere on the table cloth. You can play Easy, Medium, or Hard versions of the game and earn 1 KinzCash for each 5 points you win.

Polar Plunge

Just about everyone can master Polar Plunge, which involves taking a cute polar bear down a mountainside on a little sled. Use the arrow keys to speed up or down—the left arrow slows the sled down and the right arrow speeds it up—while the up arrow key makes the bear jump. This is important because trees and other obstacles appear in his path that he needs to jump over.

The longer you keep him moving down the hill, the more KinzCash you earn. If he falls off the sled, your turn is over.

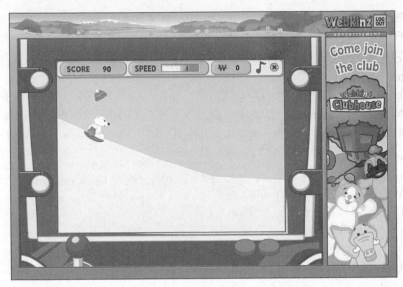

Polar Plunge is a great game for younger Webkinz owners, where the object is to avoid obstacles in the bear's path down the hill.

Pumpkin Patch Protector

In Pumpkin Patch Protector, you are the scarecrow in charge of scaring off pesky birds that fly in and try and steal the pumpkins on the ground. Your weapon is a water hose, which you squirt by moving your mouse to point the nozzle at a crow and then clicking the left mouse button. If you aim properly, you squirt the bird, and it will retreat. If it gets all the way down to the ground, however, it will have the chance to fly away with a pumpkin; and when it has one, you can't squirt it down.

According to Grant

"You can use the red target to aim a little ahead of where the bird is flying, and usually, you can hit them that way."

Quizzy's Word Challenge

Just as Quizzy's Question Corner is educational, so is Quizzy's Word Challenge, which involves making words out of letters on a board. However, you must start on the outer ring of letters and work your way into the center as you spell out words. Because you can't just pick letters from anywhere on the board, it gets a little tricky. If you can use the center letter, you get bonus points.

You earn points for each letter used, with the value increasing the further inside the board you move—the center tile is the highest value. You are also given a bonus word that earns you big points if you can make it.

Your goal is to earn as many points as you can from making 10 words, with an initial point goal of 80 points; that number increases as you move on to later rounds. If you don't hit your point goal, the game is over.

Tip

If you get stuck and just can't see any words you can make, hit the Shuffle button to get some new letters. You can do this three times, but after that, it will cost five points.

Tile Towers

The object of Tile Towers is to remove all the tiles stacked on the board by matching animal faces. Click the two matching tiles with your mouse, and they immediately disappear.

However, in addition to having matching faces, the tiles might not have tiles touching at the top or touching on the left *and* right. So you should start by looking at tiles on the outer edges that are less likely to have tiles above them or on the left and right. If you seem to be stumped, the game highlights two matching tiles to give you a hint.

If you're stuck, click Shuffle, and the tiles rearrange. If you run out of moves or out of time, the game ends. You get 1 KinzCash for every 20 points.

There are three variations of Tile Towers: the Quick game is faster, but there are fewer points at stake; the Classic game is the standard; and the Target version's goal is to remove the purple tiles.

Tulip Trouble 2

Tulip Trouble 2 is a little like the arcade game Whack-a-Mole, if you've ever played that. The object in Whack-a-Mole is to bash the moles that pop up out of holes. For every one you hit, you get points.

In Tulip Trouble 2, instead of moles, you click tulips to release good fairies that are hidden inside. It's a simple matching game—click tulips that light up and reveal the profile of a fairy head. The more fairies you release, the more points you earn. The more points you earn, the better your chances of moving to the next level. If you don't release enough fairies, however, the game ends.

Keep an eye out for the bad fairies that try to spoil your game.

Wacky Zingoz

To do well at Wacky Zingoz, you need to have excellent hand-eye coordination. Zingoz are little, yellow creatures that like to be batted around by their friends the Zangoz. You get five attempts during the game to help Zangoz bat his friend Zingoz far down the field like a baseball. With good aim and power, you can make him fly far and earn lots of points.

According to Grant _____

"Click on the Zangoz and then click your mouse about one second later, and you'll hit the Zingoz onto the field, where you can see the total distance measured."

Wacky's Bullseye Batter

If you like baseball, you may love Wacky's Bullseye Batter, where the object of the game is to help Zangoz, the hitter, smash the ball thrown to him and hit the target. It's kind of a cross between baseball and darts, actually.

To help Zangoz hit accurately, you move your mouse to line up the target with the incoming ball. If you're successful, Zangoz connects with the ball, and it goes flying into the target. If you don't, he either strikes out or hits a foul ball. And just like in baseball, if you get too many of either, "yer out."

Timing and hand-eye coordination are everything in this game, just as in baseball.

Wheel of Wow

The Wheel of Wow is that once-a-day spin you get for KinzCash and special treats. Just click "Spin," and in a few seconds, you find out what freebie you earned. There's no strategy to be learned, just click and win.

Where's Wacky

Where's Wacky is a big game of matching cards, with the number of cards to be matched increasing at every level.

You're given a set amount of time to find all the matches, and if you do, you move on to the next level. The first round involves four cards of two matches. Then, it jumps to 6 cards, then 8, 12, and so on, getting harder and harder. One set of cards to be matched features Wacky, the cute, yellow creature, and when you find him, you get a bonus.

The faster you move, the bigger your time bonus and the more KinzCash you earn.

Wishing Well

Another of those once-a-day activities you want to be sure and take advantage of, the Wishing Well allows you five spins. Each spin earns you more and more KinzCash potentially, depending on which shapes appear together on screen. After five spins, you need to wait until tomorrow to spin again. Simply click "Make a Wish" and the fun begins.

Zacky's Quest

Zacky's Quest is a lot like the arcade game Frogger. The object is to move little Zacky through several obstacles to reach five caves, each of which contains pieces of a map he needs to put together. To reach the five caves, Zacky needs to cross a river by jumping onto moving logs, then avoid Zangoz who are marching around the garden, then cross a road, more Zangoz, another river, and then enter a cave. The next round, he does the same thing but in less time and can only enter one of the remaining caves. After he does that, he moves to the next stage, with four stages in all.

Tip

Every time you see a gold coin, such as on a log or in the garden, pick it up and earn a 1 KinzCash bonus.

In addition to the Zangoz he needs to avoid, Zacky also needs to stay out of the water, not get run over by a car, and not get picked up by the birds flying overhead. If he eats 50 vegetables, which are growing in the gardens, he can earn an extra try.

Zingoz Bounce

The object of Zingoz Bounce is simple—use your mouse to keep the red Zingoz off the ground by clicking it. It's a lot like keeping a red balloon off the floor by flicking it with your fingers. And that's what you need to do here—click the red Zingoz to keep it in the air and not on the ground. You get points for the length of time you keep it airborne.

You get five tries at keeping the Zingoz in the air, and after the fifth time you drop him—and you will drop him, trust us—the game is over.

Zingoz Bounce n' Burst

The main characters in Zingoz Bounce n' Burst are Livingston the Lion, who tries to tickle big, blue puffballs called Zingoz. The Zingoz bounce around, potentially on Livingston, and he needs to use the arrow keys to move left and right and the Spacebar to shoot out ropes with feathers that tickle the Zingoz and cause them to split and shrink in size.

Some Powerup tools can help you: the clock freezes all the Zingoz for a few seconds, so you can tickle them until they burst; the round glass serves as a shield that can protect you from a bouncing Zingoz; and the blob-shaped Powerup causes all the Zingoz to giggle and burst, instantly bringing you to the next level.

> **Tip**
>
> The key to success with Zingoz Bounce n' Burst is super speedy pecking on the keyboard's Spacebar. The faster you depress the Spacebar, the more quickly ticklers are shot out to shrink the Zingoz.

Two types of ticklers can also be helpful. The double feather tickler allows you to tickle and burst two Zingoz at once. And the Plunger Tickler, which has a toilet plunger at the end, sticks to the ceiling until a Zingoz runs into it or you press the Spacebar.

Zingoz Pie Throw

Zingoz Pie Throw is a fun game involving pie throwing at little purple Zingoz, who come to try and throw a pie at you. Use the red target to line up your pie, and then click on your mouse to throw it at a Zingoz marching toward you. The more Zingoz you hit with pies, the higher your score. And once you've cleaned the field of Zingoz, you move on to the next level.

Warning

At each level, your supply of pies is replenished by the Pie Zingoz, who comes across the screen to deliver them. You do *not* want to hit him, or he stops bringing pies.

The closer the Zingoz advance, the easier it is to hit them, but the better their chances of hitting you, which you don't want. After the first few levels, you also see airborne Zingoz trying to fly in and throw pies at you. You need to shoot them down to avoid being pie'd.

After you are hit by three pies, the game is over.

Zingoz Pop

In Zingoz Pop, the object is to shoot bubbles out of a bubble machine and line up three or more like-colored bubbles, which causes them all to pop. You want to pop all the bubbles in the tank this way, using your left and right arrow keys to guide the pointer and the up arrow to actually propel the bubble. When you pop all the bubbles, you go to the next level.

At the beginning, you can choose one of four special powers to be made available to you. You have to pop the glowing bubble to use the special power, such as popping all the bubbles of a certain color.

What makes it a challenge is that the bubble machine shows the next bubble to be thrown, not the current one, so you need to remember what the next color is to properly line the colors up. Otherwise, you get a tank of multicolored bubbles, none of which have popped.

If the tank fills, your game is done.

Tournaments

It's fun to play Arcade games alone, but when your child masters a game, she might want to compete against other kids. To do that, you participate in a tournament, which is found in the Things to Do menu bar.

Many of the games in the Arcade can also be played against other people. Many of these tournaments are not live, head-to-head competition, but rather "best of" games during a particular time period, such as a day.

Competing in a Tournament

When you decide to join a tournament, you might compete against 9 people or 14 people or even 19 people; it just depends on that particular tournament. And each of your competitors isn't necessarily playing at the same time you are—it's kind of like a timed race. You play the game and your score is noted. Then, after all your competitors finish their game, the person with the highest score wins the tournament.

Just like in the Arcade, you can choose from dozens of tournaments to compete in, including some that are only found here.

Getting Started

To enter a tournament, click "Tournament Arena" from the "Things to Do' menu bar. You see a list of all the possible tournament games, which are actually most of the Arcade games.

Click the game you want to play; then click the friend from your friend list (which is shown on the screen) you want to compete against or ask Webkinz to "Find Me an Opponent," which is always an option. Or choose "Quick Tournaments" to participate in a group event. Then click which prize you want to play for and click "Join Tournament" to start playing. Tournaments with more people participating offer larger KinzCash prizes.

Your score is compared against the scores of all the other players to determine the tournament winner.

Clever Competitions

In addition to offering Arcade games for more than one player, there are also a number of games that can only be played here in the Tournament Arena. These include:

◆ **Trading Card Challenge**—You can play a live version of Trading Card Challenge if you've collected 50 of your own Webkinz trading cards, but this online game requires no real cards at all. The object is to win four challenges before your opponent. You are dealt cards, and then draw or act on the cards you have in order to beat the other player.

Webkinz offers step-by-step guidance for playing this game, which is recommended for ages 8 and up, at www.webkinz.com/ TCG_howtoplay.html.

◆ **Trading Card Mix n' Match**—Mix n' Match is more like a traditional game of Fish or Crazy 8's, with the object being to collect four online sets of either mixed or matched sets of cards. A set consists of four cards, with a mixed set including four cards with nothing in common and a matched set including four cards with at least one thing in common, such as they are all action cards or all Arcade games.

The first player to collect four sets wins.

◆ **Checkers**—Webkinz Checkers is just like traditional checkers, only it is played online. You move your pieces across the board in an attempt to reach the opponent's side without being jumped and captured. Any pieces that do reach the other side are King'd, by adding another piece on top, and can then move in any direction.

The last player on the board wins the game and the bulk of the tournament winnings.

◆ **DiceKinz**—DiceKinz is an online board game that involves rolling your dice to move, with the larger objective being to knock out your opponent's Run dice. At the same time, you want to protect your own Run dice, using the powers that are shown on your dice to do this. Whatever number of Run points you have showing on your dice are the number of squares you move on the board.

This is another more advanced game for older children and you may want to have your child watch the Tutorial to understand the subtleties.

◆ **Dogbcard's Bathtub Battles**—The electronic version of Battleship, this game pits one pirate (you) against another in an effort to figure out where the other pirate's ships are hidden on the board. During each turn you can fire on your opponent's board in the hopes of landing on a part of her ship. When you discover one, you shoot around it in order to completely blow it up.

The first player to reveal all of her opponent's five ships wins.

◆ **Kinz Pinz Bowling**—Just like Webkinz Mini Golf, Kinz Pinz Bowling is a virtual version of the real activity, complete with an opponent to bowl against. How well you line up your ball with the pins and the power with which you propel the ball will determine whether you get a spare, or barely knock any down. It takes technique to get good at this game, so don't be disappointed if you don't win the first game.

◆ **Link'D**—If you've ever played the game Connect Four, where you drop coin-sized circles to try and block your opponent from getting four of the circles across, down, or diagonally, you'll immediately understand Link'D. It's a two-person game that even the youngest Webkinz owner can play.

◆ **Quizzy's WhizKinz**—Anyone who has had luck answering Quizzy's questions should try this tournament game, which pits two opponents against each other in a battle of wits. Well, actually, it's more of a battle to answer 20 questions correctly to earn the high score. Whoever does wins the prize money.

◆ **Rock Paper Scissors**—This is the electronic version of that age-old favorite, which is typically played with opposing fists. As always, rock beats scissors, scissors cuts paper, and paper covers rock. Knowing these basic rules, you try and outwit your competitor.

The first player to win three times is the champion.

◆ **Webkinz Chef Challenge**—Seemingly modeled after the *Iron Chef* television show, Webkinz Chef Challenge pits your child against another in a battle to concoct the most delicious dish to please the judges. Each player is asked to combine up to three ingredients from a list of six to create a specific dish, such as Speckled Sing Songs or Wheezy-Breezalumps. Then the three Webkinz judges sample the virtual cuisine and award points for taste and creativity. Each round has a winner with the champion being the first to win three rounds.

> **Warning**
>
> Do not try and leave a game before points have been awarded or you'll end up with zero KinzCash for your efforts. Wait until the winner has been declared to be sure you get some of the prize money.

◆ **Webkinz SuperModelz**—Another game mimicking a TV hit is Webkzinz SuperModelz, which has two players each choose a model and three articles of clothing—a shirt, pants, and hat—from a selection of six or seven each. The SuperModelz judges then evaluate each outfit, awarding points according to their preferences. There is a winner for each round, with the first player to win three rounds becoming the overall winner.

The Least You Need to Know

◆ You can play with your pet in its room, play interactive games, decorate the room, cook, bath your pet, or invite friends over.

◆ Arcade games help develop keyboarding and memory skills, in addition to earning your child KinzCash.

◆ Some Arcade games pay more KinzCash more quickly, so pay attention to how many points it takes to earn 1 KinzCash.

◆ Playing against other Webkinz owners in tournaments is a fun way to compare your skills against others.

Chapter 4

Educational Activities

In This Chapter

- ◆ Learning that looks like fun
- ◆ Matching games that improve memory
- ◆ Reinforcing word formation skills
- ◆ Introducing useful facts and figures

Although fun and games are at the heart of Webkinz® World, the emphasis is on learning and skill-building, too. What's great is that kids don't know they're learning— they're just enjoying themselves.

While playing Arcade games or competing in tournaments, your child can develop keyboarding skills, improve spelling and word formation abilities, strengthen memory and focus, and build a solid knowledge base of math, the arts, social studies, language, health, and science facts—not to mention the counting and money management skills they pick up through earning and spending KinzCash® to care for their Webkinz pet.

Some of the best places to challenge your child's skills are in Quizzy's Question Corner and Quizzy's Word Challenge, in the Employment Office, and in the Arcade on games such as Lunch

Letters and Where's Wacky. This chapter looks at these games and kids' educational opportunities.

Quizzy's

Quizzy's two games—Word Challenge and Question Corner—are entirely educational, but maybe your child will play them anyway.

Quizzy's Word Challenge is in the Arcade, on the Things to Do menu bar, and Quizzy's Question Corner has its own button on the Things to Do menu bar.

Word Challenge

Word Challenge is best for children who are already reading, because the object of the game is to form words from letters on the screen. It's hard to come up with words if you cannot recognize them, so we recommend it for ages 6 and up.

The good news is that every 7 points earned at Word Challenge yields 1 KinzCash, so it takes little time to boost your KinzCash account.

Tip

You can quickly earn some extra KinzCash by clicking the Calendar Trivia icon in the bottom-right corner of the Quizzy's Question Challenge home page. When there, you can answer questions posed in the past, even previous months. Just click earlier months and then click each day to see what that day's questions were.

To play the game, you make 10 words out of the letters provided, with points given for each letter you use, just like in Scrabble. The twist with this game is that you must work from the outer edge of the square of letters, moving in as you form the words. You can form a word using all the letters in one tier, or you can start at the outer edge and work your way in toward the center. If you use the center-most letter as the last letter in your word, you get bonus points.

Warning _____

You get a bonus word for extra points if you can form it using the letters in the square. However, not every letter is available in each round, so you want to start trying immediately to put it together. In many cases, the letters you need are only available the first couple of times you put words together. (The set of letters changes after each word you make.) You can also scramble the letters up to three times during the game without any point deduction.

Question Corner

Although Quizzy's Question Corner also requires reading ability to understand the questions and four multiple choice answers, parents can help younger children by reading the questions and answers aloud.

Quizzy's has modules of 50 questions on a wide variety of subjects—the arts, social studies, health, math, language, and science—for children ages 5 to 6, 7 to 8, 9 to 10, 11 to 12, and 13+. There are also questions for "Everyone" in different categories—kid's world, pop culture, animals, sports, and fun facts.

Each Quizzy's question is worth 5 KinzCash and is asked in a multiple choice format with four possible answers. If you don't answer within the first few seconds, one of the answers is cleared from the screen, then another, until you're left with the correct answer. Each time a possible answer is eliminated, however, your potential KinzCash earnings go down. And if you guess wrong or don't guess at all, your earnings for that question are zero.

According to Grant _____

"I usually answer the questions for younger kids when I want to earn KinzCash quicker."

When the question's answer is revealed, either because you guessed correctly or Webkinz told you the answer, another quick sentence appears on the screen with a random factoid about the previous question. It's just another little learning opportunity that the creators of Webkinz sneak in.

Tip

Interested in finding out who the top 10 Quizzy's Champions are?
Or the folks who have answered the most Quizzy's questions ever?
Just click the Quizzy's Champions trophy and the list appears. Each time
you answer 50 questions in a category, you earn a virtual sticker in your
Quizzy's album, which you can view any time on the main Quizzy's
page.

Employment Office

Another area of the Webkinz website devoted to skill-building is the
Employment Office, which is found on the Things to Do menu bar.
The Employment Office provides opportunities to try out various
jobs every eight hours. If you successfully complete a task, you earn
KinzCash and a possible promotion to the next level, where the pay is
better but the tasks are a notch harder.

Fence Painting

The challenge with fence painting is getting each of the five fence
posts covered with the correct paint color—red, blue, green, or
yellow—based on the original pattern presented at the start of the job.

A painted fence is shown, and then you need to paint the next blank
fence to match the first one. If you do it correctly, another fence is
shown that you need to match as well, and so on, until you paint five
fences.

The painted fence slats are shown only for a few seconds before your
task needs to begin, so look carefully. Then use your mouse to move
your paintbrush to the first color and then onto the fence to be painted.
Next, move your brush to the can of paint for the second fence slat,
then onto the fence, and so on. When you finish the last piece of fence,
you find out if you did it correctly.

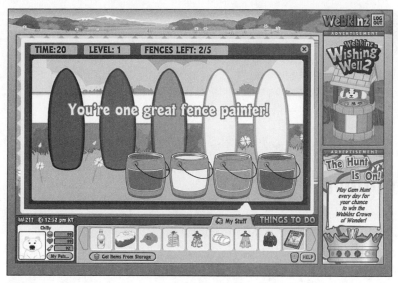

The task of fence painting is easy enough for virtually any age player.

Tip

Not sure which level you're on at each job? Just click your resumé positioned in the lower-right side of the Employment Office screen by Ms. T. (Tabby) Von Meow, and you can see which jobs you've done, which level you're on, and how much KinzCash you can earn for completing each task.

Shoe Store Clerk

Working as a shoe store clerk involves matching 10 pairs of shoes within the allotted time. The job requires a good memory and speed to match up the scattered shoes, sneakers, slippers, and boots. If you can beat the clock and match all the shoes during three tests, you earn credit for the task.

When the clock starts ticking, you open two shoe boxes at a time. If they are a match, the shoes stay on screen. If they are not, the box top goes back on to hide the shoes, and you try two other boxes.

After you complete the tests on three separate occasions, you move to the next level, where you can earn more KinzCash each time you work.

Tip

To help you more easily remember where the different colored shoes are, work methodically down each column, repeating the names of the colors to yourself out loud. It is easier to quickly find shoes' mates if you have a system for remembering past shoes.

Dr. Quack's Assistant

As Dr. Quack's assistant, you need to match the appropriate medical treatment available to each patient's ailment or injury. Sometimes, patients come in individually, and other times two or three at a time, which makes it challenging to treat them accurately and quickly and in the order in which they arrived.

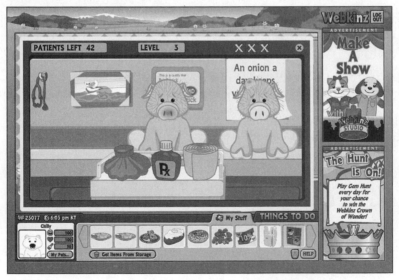

Kids love to help animals feel better, and this is an encouraging way to do it.

Keep It Simple

As of the time of writing this, there are only two levels—Easy and Medium—but a Hard level is in the works.

The three possible treatments are an ice bag for a bump, a bottle of cough medicine for a red nose, and a roll of bandages for a scrape or scratch. When a patient appears on the screen with one of the conditions, you drag the treatment over on top of the hurt area, such as the head, leg, or nose to make it feel better.

When you are successful, your patient might giggle in delight and disappear. If you get any wrong, a red "x" will appear at the top of the screen. Three x's in a row and your job ends.

Grocery Clerk

Depending on your child's age, he might have grocery clerk as one of the available jobs. To tackle the grocery clerk job, you need to have completed 50 Quizzy's math questions to qualify.

As a grocery clerk, the object is to move all the grocery items on the bottom conveyor belt up onto the conveyor belt at the top of the screen, so they can be bagged. The items on the bottom conveyor belt include colorful food such as apples, oranges, asparagus bunches, cupcakes, lollipops, ice cream cones, and pretzels, among others. The top conveyor belt consists of white cut-out shapes that match the shapes of the food on the bottom conveyor.

Using your mouse, drag a food item from the bottom conveyor and place it exactly on top of the blank shape on the top one. The top conveyor belt moves more quickly than the bottom, so it's hard to keep up.

> **Tip**
>
> You can click a food item and drag it halfway between the conveyor belts until it appears on the top one and then drop it into place.

You're timed and unless you successfully bag enough food before time runs out, your career as a grocery clerk might be short-lived. At least for the next eight hours, then you can try, try again.

Flooring Assistant

To be a flooring assistant, you need to answer 50 of Quizzy's social studies questions. After you take the job, you need to recreate five tricky flooring designs using six two-colored tiles.

You're given a master design in the top right of the screen, consisting of six squares that you need to match up on the floor in the home. Each of the six squares is either solid white, solid blue, or a combination of the two with triangles inside the squares. You need to work methodically and match up each square. When you complete each design, you're given the next one. The clock is ticking down, and if you don't complete all the floors in time, you don't get credit for the job.

Piano Player

You need to answer 50 Quizzy's questions about the arts before you can apply for a job as a piano player.

If your child can watch and listen for which notes are played, she will do well as a piano player.

After you qualify, the job of piano player requires you to repeat 10 patterns of notes played on a piano, which you do using your mouse to tap on different on-screen keys. Turn up your speakers so that you can hear the notes played, which can help recall the patterns, and watch the screen.

The first set of notes are just two in a row. But the more sets you play, the more notes are added, until you need to replicate six or more notes by the end. If you miss three of the patterns, your time in the spotlight is up.

Hamburger Cook

Working as a hamburger cook requires a good memory for patterns, because the job involves making a hamburger to match an on-screen picture of one. Five hamburgers are presented, one at a time, with different combinations of hamburger, cheese, tomatoes, and lettuce.

Watch the first hamburger made closely, to catch exactly how many layers of each component are stacked and then do exactly the same combo on your hamburger.

Working as a hamburger cook is another task that strengthens memory, as kids copy condiment layers shown on the screen.

It's not hard if you watch carefully, but it's easy to get tripped up on multiple levels of one ingredient, which are hard to spot. (It's hard to tell whether there are three or four pieces of lettuce, for example, unless you watched and counted the first burger being made.)

Gem Mining

To qualify for gem mining, you first need to have 20 different gems in your gem box.

The game begins with you getting a quick look at a stack of about 25 or 30 black rocks, some of which have colorful gems inside of them. Then the lights go out, and you can no longer see which rocks have gems and which don't.

The object in gem mining is to remember where all the gems are hiding and then pull them out using a claw and stack them in a holding tank. You don't want to pull out slag though, or you lose 2 seconds off your time. To get to some of the gems in the bottom, you might need to relocate some of the rocks out of the way.

> **Tip**
>
> When you see the screen with the gems showing, make a little map of where they are so that when the lights go out, you can quickly work to dig them out using your map.

When you find all the gems and load them in the tank, without loading slag, too, you get credit for your work.

Ms. Birdy's Assistant

Before you can apply to be Ms. Birdy's assistant, you need to have completed 100 Quizzy's language questions.

> **According to Grant**
>
> "If you go to the Employment Office before school, you can go again when you get home because eight hours will have gone by."

The challenge as Ms. Birdy's assistant is to type the words that appear on the screen as quickly as you can and as accurately as you can. Words like "care," "awards," and "honey" need to be replicated on your computer keyboard. Any mistakes as you type and 2 seconds are deducted from your total time, making it tougher to complete all the words before time runs out.

Ms. Birdy clearly needs an accurate typist to help her, so focus on getting the words spelled correctly as you type, rather than on your speed, which improves over time.

Newz Delivery

A newer employment opportunity is *Newz* delivery, where your child has to throw a newspaper onto the doorsteps of homes that have subscribed, which are green. There are other houses with red doors that you don't want to deliver to. You use the mouse to line up the newspaper with the house and then click on the mouse to throw the paper onto the doormat.

You can get up to three strikes, either for missing a door or throwing the paper onto a red door, before you're fired.

Arcade Games

All the Arcade games are fun, and a couple are even educationally oriented. Lunch Letters, where kids practice spelling and keyboarding skills, and Where's Wacky, where their memory and deductive reasoning skills are honed, are two of the strongest games.

Lunch Letters

Any child who likes typing and playing on the computer keyboard is likely to enjoy Lunch Letters, which requires typing whatever letter or series of letters fall from the sky before they hit the ground, where the school janitor sweeps them up.

You can choose from several levels, including Easy, Medium, Hard, and Very Hard, and within each of those, there are levels, starting at 1 and moving up as you complete a series of letters and words.

Lunch Letters can quickly improve your child's keyboarding skills by requiring that he types letters as they fall.

Keep It Simple

To help track your progress, you can print out a certificate at the completion of each game of Lunch Letters.

In the easiest level, you start with single letters but quickly move up to multiple-letter words mingled with the single letters, making it more challenging to type the words before they hit the ground. At the end of each round, you receive a summary of your typing speed and accuracy.

At the Very Hard level, even longer words come faster from the sky, making it tough to keep all the letters from cluttering the janitor's floor. But it's excellent practice, no matter how many levels you can get through.

Where's Wacky

Where's Wacky is a progressively harder memory challenge game, where you turn over pairs of cards featuring cute Webkinz animals and try to make a match. When you have a match, the two cards disappear, and you are left with the rest of the cards still needing matches.

Where's Wacky is a lot like the shoe store clerk challenge, except that here you match Webkinz characters and not shoes.

If you make all the matches before time is up, you move on to the next level, which is more challenging. But if time is called and you still have matches on the screen, the game is over.

Despite the educational value of Webkinz and its activities, you still want to be sure your child isn't glued to the computer too long.

Warning

As Webkinz has grown in popularity, there are now tips for cheating floating around in cyberspace. Be aware that Webkinz is watching for such activity, and if you or your child are caught trying to circumvent the system to earn a wad of KinzCash, you'll be immediately terminated from Webkinz and banned.

The Least You Need to Know

◆ All the games on Webkinz are fun, but there are plenty that reinforce basic computing, math, and age-appropriate facts, too.

◆ In addition to the Arcade games and Quizzy's, Webkinz promotes reading through its online newspaper and stories called W Tales.

◆ The Employment Office offers rotating jobs, so different kids may see different assignments on the job board.

◆ Arcade games like Lunch Letters and Where's Wacky reinforce keyboarding, spelling, and memory skills.

◆ Sometimes, answering Quizzy's questions is required before you can qualify for some jobs in the Employment Office.

Communication and Security

In This Chapter

- ◆ Understanding built-in safety features
- ◆ Talking to your pet
- ◆ Chatting with other players
- ◆ Sending and receiving mail

Webkinz® World is a great place for kids to entertain themselves, whether by playing with their pet, playing games by themselves, or testing their knowledge with Quizzy's. In addition to the many games that can be played against a virtual opponent, it is also possible to compete against, and to be friendly with, other Webkinz owners, too. However, such friendships occur only within strict boundaries set by Webkinz World.

Site Safety

The corporate parent of Webkinz, Ganz, has gone to great lengths to make playing in Webkinz World safe for children. The company has set up rigorous firewalls to try and prevent person-to-person contact beyond basic greetings and discussions. No personal information is shared—the system simply won't allow descriptive words and phrases, or numbers, to be shared inside the system, which makes it more difficult for users to know anything distinctive about each other.

Children can't share identifying information about themselves or receive it from others, which helps to prohibit any kind of unwanted contact. Unless a friend or family member provides his username directly, outside of Webkinz World, there is virtually no way that your child could find them. Likewise, others would have no way to track down your child using his username unless they learned it during regular conversation, outside of Webkinz World.

> **Keep It Simple**
>
> Parents can block their children from accessing KinzChat Plus, or even requesting permission to access it, through the Parents Area on the Webkinz home page.

Who Is Online

Although your child can compile a list of friends who play on Webkinz, some of the usernames in her phone list might be of people she has never met but who have asked to be friends following an online tournament where they had contact. Most of the names, however, will be from school or neighborhood friends and family members. Either way, there is no way for either kid—the new friend or your child—to know anything about the other person, which makes it safe.

Webkinz World was designed for children ages 6 to 13, but it does not prevent others who are younger or older from playing along. So do not assume the person you might be playing checkers with is someone your own age.

You can keep track of who your child converses with by looking at his friends list, which displays on his Webkinz cell phone.

Color Zones

So that Webkinz servers don't get overloaded, people on the website are divided into different colored zones. There is no significance to the different color names; they are just a way to separate all the Webkinz owners.

Your friends might be in Webkinz World, but you need to both be in the same color zone to chat.

If you decide you'd like to talk to a friend in Webkinz World, you first need to go to the same color zone he is in, which we talk about in the section on KinzChat.

Adding Friends to Your List

If you don't currently have any friends in your chat list, which is shown on the cell phone in the bottom right of your screen, you can still play and have plenty of fun in Webkinz World. If you want to chat with friends from school or from your street, you need to add them to your list.

Adding friends is easy if you know their screen names. A *screen name* is the name used when you sign in to Webkinz World. To add friends, click your cell phone to open it. Then click the "Power" button to turn it on and click "Add" to add a name. Type the friend's user name to add her to your chat list and click "Add."

A note is immediately sent to your friend to ask if it's okay for her to be added to your chat list. The next time she logs in to Webkinz World she'll see the note and can respond "yes" or "no" to your invitation. If she says "yes," her name will appear on your chat list shortly.

Tip

If you're new to Webkinz and don't have friends yet, go to the Tournament Arena, which is on the Things to Do menu bar, and choose a game to play. Then click "Find an Opponent," which means that Webkinz World will find another person to play you. After you finish your game, you might decide to ask the person to be your friend. If he says "yes," add him to your chat list. This is still a secure process because you know absolutely nothing about the other child, and he knows nothing about your child, nor can he with Webkinz' built-in safeguards.

Talking with Other Players

Webkinz owners can chat with each other and send messages through the system, which is closely controlled and monitored. At no time can players send revealing or inappropriate information.

Clubhouse

The Clubhouse is a meeting place for Webkinz owners, just like a real clubhouse. Except this one has many different rooms you can choose to hang out in. First, you need to enter either KinzChat or KinzChat Plus.

Your child can talk with friends using KinzChat, which allows only certain phrases to be used, or more flexible KinzChat Plus, which permits freehand typing but prohibits certain words.

When you enter the clubhouse, you can then head to one of several different theme rooms where you can interact with other pet owners. The rooms include the following:

◆ Party room

◆ Games room

◆ Go Fish room

◆ Link'd room

◆ Collector room

◆ Girls Rule room

◆ Sports room

◆ Exercise room

◆ Reading room

◆ Garden yard

Inside, each room is decorated in a style to match its name. Within the room, however, you see a list of numbered rooms, such as Garden Room 03 or Garden Room 18. Each of these is a Garden Room, but there are so many people who want to go there that Webkinz had to create copies of the original room. So choose one of the numbered rooms and enter.

> **Tip**
>
> Before you choose a room, you might want to click "Find My Friends" to see where your buddies are congregating. Then click the room where they're hanging out.

> **According to Grant**
>
> "My Webkinz likes bouncing on the trampolines in the Garden Room the best."

To the right of each room name is a fraction representing how many people are in the room and what its capacity is. The number will be "some number"/10 because there can be no more than 10 people per room. If there are already 10 people in a room, it will say "Full." You have to wait for someone to exit before you can go in.

After you're in the room, you can go to a different room by clicking the "Switch Rooms" button that brings you back to the page listing all your options.

KinzChat

KinzChat is the technology used to speak to other Webkinz owners in Webkinz World. You use it when you talk on the phone, when you visit friends, and when you hang out in the Clubhouse.

KinzChat allows kids to speak to others using predefined words and sentences, but they cannot type their own messages. KinzChat Plus, which requires a parent's permission to use, does allow a child to type his own messages, but the messages cannot contain descriptors or information that would help someone else contact him.

When you talk with friends, you use the "Ask," "Say," and "Rap" buttons to communicate. To ask a question, use the Ask button, which has a list of common questions you might want to ask. To respond to a question, you can use Say or Rap. Rap has shorter responses and acronyms, like "LOL." Choose the question or answer you want to give and then scroll and click it. Then wait for a reply from your friend.

Warning

Check the different colored zones on your KinzChat phone, in the lower-right corner of your computer screen, to see which are available. If four faces show in one zone, it is full, and you need to choose a different zone.

KinzChat Plus

The big difference between KinzChat and KinzChat Plus is that kids can type their own responses in KinzChat Plus, rather than selecting from a limited list of questions and answers. However, even in KinzChat Plus, which you need your parents approval to use, there is a limited number of words you can use to form sentences.

Keep It Simple

If your child uses forbidden words in KinzChat Plus, the words will turn red on the screen so that he can try and find an acceptable alternative, if there is one. If not, the message simply won't be transmitted.

Talking to Your Pet

Regardless of whether your friends are around, your Webkinz is always there, always interested in talking with you. Your pet will often tell you how it feels or cheer you on when you do really well at a game. And you can also respond.

To speak to your pet, you need to be in My Room. And when there, you see a button in the lower-left corner that reads, "Speak to your pet." Click that, and you see a list of possible things you could ask your pet, like "How are you feeling?" or "Anything happen while I was gone?" Or you can tell it how much you care, such as "You're such a good pet."

Each time you tell your Webkinz something, you see a response back, which appears in a little bubble above your pet's head.

KinzPost

If friends aren't in Webkinz World and you want to send them a note, the easiest way is to mail a message through KinzPost, which is on the Things to Do menu.

KinzPost permits only certain messages to be sent, which are selected from a list provided.

To send a message via KinzPost, click KinzPost and then decide whether you want to send a gift or a note. A gift is usually something little from the W Shop, but it can be something big—perhaps a piece of furniture you no longer want or that you know your friend would love. And a note is a message without any kind of gift.

Send a Note

To send a note, first choose a topic from the list of topics available:

◆ About Webkinz World

◆ Birthday

- Friendship
- Get in touch
- Good luck
- Have a great day
- Just because
- Meet me in Webkinz World
- Thank you

After you choose a general topic for your message, you can choose a specific message to go with it. For each topic, you'll be given a list of one-line messages you can pick and choose from.

For example, if you're sending a birthday note, you might choose one of the following:

- Wishing you the best birthday EVER!
- I hope your birthday is wonderful!
- Happy birthday, my friend!

And if those don't exactly work for you, there are several others available.

Or if you're sending a "Get in touch" message, you can choose from among the following (as well as a few others):

- How are you doing? E-mail me and let me know!
- Long time no talk … call me!
- Hey! Give me a call!

After choosing your message, click "Next," and you'll be given a preview of your note. You can also jazz up your note with some stickers, which are shown on the left side of the page. Click the right arrow next to each of the sticker pictures to choose the shape and color sticker you want.

If you want to send the note on plain stationery, it will cost 1 KinzCash® to mail. But if you want a fancier design, just click the right arrow to see all your options—everything from colorful crayons to dancing Webkinz animals, at prices starting at 5 KinzCash and ranging all the way up to 50.

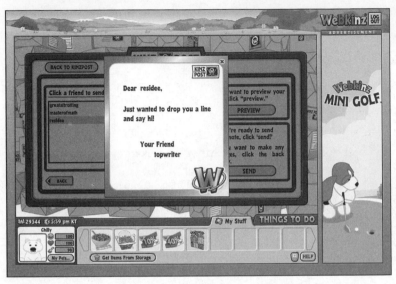

Sending a note isn't hard to do and Webkinz leads you through the process step-by-step.

On the next screen, you are shown a list of all the friends on your friends list, so you can choose to whom to send the note. Of course, these names are screen names—you never see real names or any identifying information about your online buddies. Click the friend's user name and then either click "Send," to send it, or "Preview," so you can check out what the finished product will look like before sending it.

After you click "Send," you see your note flying through cyberspace to your friend. At that point, you can click "Back to KinzPost" to send another note or head somewhere else in Webkinz World.

Send a Gift

Sending a gift to a friend is similar to sending a note, except you can choose to wrap it in colorful paper and a bow, for an extra fee, of course, and it costs more to mail—15 KinzCash for each item you ship.

To send a gift, click that option within KinzPost, under the Things to Do menu bar. Then choose up to three things from your dock—food, furniture, or some other treat you own—and drag it from your dock up into the box that's open on the screen.

Next, choose wrapping paper—the fancier it is, the more it costs. You can use plain brown wrapping paper, which costs nothing extra, or colored paper, which costs 10 KinzCash extra, or really, really special sparkly paper, which costs 60 KinzCash.

According to Grant

"I like to send my friends packages just for fun, and it's great when they send me stuff, too. I even got a scooter once!"

Choose the friend you want to send it to and the message you want to attach. After you do that, click send, and it will be on its way.

Keep It Simple

Your child will see several reminders that sending a gift to a friend does not mean she will get anything in return. It's a gift, which means she should do it without the expectation that her friend might send something back.

The next time your friend arrives in his room, he will see he has mail with the little letter icon on the screen.

Visiting Friends Virtually

In addition to chatting with your friends and sending them notes via KinzPost, you can also go and visit their Webkinz home or invite them over to visit yours.

Inviting Friends Over

To invite a Webkinz pet over to play with your pet, first go to My Room. Then turn on your cell phone by clicking it to enlarge it and then clicking "Power," which turns it on.

If anyone on your friends list is on Webkinz at the same time and in the same color zone, their faces will be green and smiling. Because so many kids use Webkinz World at any one time, they are divided into different groups, or zones, identified by colors—purple, light blue, green, yellow, orange, light green, amber, dark blue, teal, pink, and red.

You can invite friends over to play in your room and to enjoy your pet's toys.

Warning

If you decide to leave Webkinz World, make sure you send your friends home first, using the little button on your screen, so they don't hang out without you there.

If you see a red face with a colored bar around it, you know that friend is not in the same zone and is not available to chat. The colored bar around him tells you which zone he was last in, in case you want to go to that zone to see if he's around. If he is in another zone, his red face will turn green when you enter.

Look for your friend's username on your friends list on the phone to see if it shows a smiling green face next to it. Click it, and you will both hear a little voice say "Yoohoo."

Then click the word "Invite," which is in the middle of your cell phone, and a note will be sent to your friend. In the middle of his computer screen he sees, "[Your username] has invited you over. Would you like to visit his house?" He can then click "Yes" or "No."

If he clicks "Yes," his Webkinz pet will immediately be transported to your doorstep, and you'll hear the doorbell ring.

Tip

If you don't want to be bothered with invitations to visit while you're playing in Webkinz World, click the yellow "Do Not Disturb" button on your phone. When you're open to invitations, click "Do Not Disturb" again to have it cleared. Likewise, if you see a friend's name in yellow, it means he put his "Do Not Disturb" notice up.

When you leave Webkinz World, log out so that your friends know you left.

Going to Visit

When you receive an invitation on screen to go visit one of your friends, you can choose whether to accept. Click "Yes" if you want to go check out a friend's room(s) or "No" if you're just not in the mood to socialize.

Tip

When you visit a friend or she comes visit you, use the Speak function to have a conversation with her. You simply choose the phrase you want to use—a question or a comment—and then select it. It appears over your pet's head on the screen. Your friend can then decide whether to respond and chat with you.

The Least You Need to Know

◆ Kids cannot send personal information to each other.

◆ By typing in the screen names of your friends, you can communicate with them via KinzChat while they're in Webkinz World.

◆ Even KinzChat Plus has a restrictive dictionary, which permits only certain words to be used in correspondence with friends. KinzChat does not allow original messages to be typed.

◆ If your friend's name appears in green, he's online. If it's yellow, he asked you not to disturb him, and if it's read, he's not around.

◆ You can also send friends a quick note or a gift, though you can't send KinzCash.

◆ If you invite friends over to visit your Webkinz room, be sure and send them back home before you leave.

Chapter 6

Other Fun Things to Do Online

In This Chapter

◆ Making Webkinz® movies

◆ Choosing actors

◆ Coming up with stories

◆ Watching the movies

One of the coolest activities in Webkinz World isn't an Arcade or tournament game; it's a movie studio. Kids can actually produce their own animated movies using Webkinz characters, backgrounds, and production equipment and then show them to their friends and family.

In addition to fostering creativity, the Webkinz Movie Studio also builds computing knowledge, logical thought, and writing skills, as children think through what they want to occur in each movie scene. This chapter will help you help to your child learn to make his or her own movies.

Webkinz Studio

If your child has an interest in movies or wants to stay current on the latest and greatest Webkinz activities, you definitely want to show her Webkinz Studio.

Webkinz Studio is the program that runs the movie production module. It's available in the W Shop, in the Toys and Books category, for 1,000 KinzCash®. Yes, it's a bit pricey, but it does more—and is more multifaceted—than most other interactive elements on the site.

Webkinz Studio is a software product that looks like a miniature movie production studio you set up in your pet's room.

To start, head to your Webkinz's room and drag the Webkinz Studio from your dock up into the room, just like any other piece of furniture or toy. It appears on the floor and looks like a tiny movie set. To start the program, move your pet over next to it and then click the studio itself.

Making Movies

When the studio program starts, a new screen pops up that asks if you want to either

- ◆ Add New Actors/Sets

- ◆ Make a New Show

If you already created a movie, you can watch it by clicking "My Old Movies" in the lower-right corner.

If making a new movie, think of a title for your movie and type it into the space in the center of your computer screen. If you can, keep it short—just a few words. A title that is a play on words is always a good choice.

When you click to enter your movie title, you'll be asked to start making decisions about what your movie looks like. First, choose the background setting. The basic studio program offers you two choices: city buildings or farm land. Next, choose the color of blue sky you prefer· deep blue or turquoise.

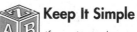 **Keep It Simple**

If you're editing a movie you started previously, you can click "Add New Actors/ Sets" and then add to it.

Expanding Your Creative Options

If you feel restricted by the lack of set options, you can always buy a different background in the W Shop, in Toys and Books. The following complete background packages are available for 250 KinzCash each:

- ◆ Final Frontier playset—moon and starry sky

- ◆ Land of Candy playset—candy galore

- ◆ Medieval playset—castle and evening sky

- ◆ Haunted House playset—spooky house and night

- ◆ Pirate Lore playset—pirate ship and ocean

- ◆ Rocking World Tour playset—rock and roll stage

- ◆ Wild West playset—desert and dusk

After you settle on your background, your next challenge is to choose mood music. Your options include the following:

◆ Action packed

◆ Comedy 1

◆ Comedy 2

◆ Dramatic

◆ Romantic

Click each one and then click the "Play" button to listen to the basic tempo to see which music best matches the overall pace of your show. If it's a silly show, one of the first three types of music might work best, but if it's sad or scary, the dramatic tune might support the storyline better. And if you create a love story, the romantic melody is probably a good choice.

On the next screen, you need to choose two actors to act in your TV movie. You are shown two actors at the start—a puppy and a kitten— that are your only two options with the basic studio package. Drag the photo of each of them into one of the "film cells." When you do, the word "Hired" appears across their faces.

Hiring More Actors

If you feel like these two actors are not the best for your particular story, you can buy additional actors to feature in your movie. Each one comes dressed appropriately for different types of scenes and movies. All cost 150 KinzCash each:

◆ Ancient Mummy actor

◆ Bad Fairy actor

◆ Country Cowgirl actor

◆ Froggenstein actor

◆ Good Fairy actor

◆ Night Witch actor

◆ Plunderin' Pirate actor

◆ Pop Princess actor

◆ Pretty Pink Princess actor

◆ Robot actor

◆ Valiant Knight actor

Keep It Simple _____

To add new characters or sets, you first buy them in the W Shop. Start the Webkinz Studio and click the button for "Add New Actors/ Sets," which appears on the first screen. Drag-and-drop your actors or sets into the boxes provided. They immediately appear in the window as possible selections for you to choose from.

After you select your two actors, click "Next" to move to your next decision.

With all the pieces of your movie chosen, you now need to start putting them together in a way that makes sense for the viewer. Your next task is to choose the camera angle for the first scene. Your movie can be up to 15 scenes long, but no longer, so keep this in mind as you begin filming. Of course, it can be shorter, too.

The possible camera angles for all scenes include the following:

◆ Both actors shown, far away

◆ Both actors shown, up close

◆ Actor 1 only

◆ Actor 2 only

After you click your selection, you see your actors in place against the background and sky you chose.

If that looks good, you can now begin work on the *dialogue*—what the actors say to each other. You can either have Actor 1 or Actor 2 say the first sentence, and when the first is done, click the tab for the second and type his response to the first actor's remarks.

According to Grant _____

"I like making silly movies. I make the actors shake and look scary while they talk."

It's exciting to see all your decisions come together in the first scene of your movie.

Next, choose the emotion you'd like each actor to display. You can choose from several:

- Normal
- Happy
- Sad
- Scared

- Angry
- Suspicious
- Sinister

The emotions are expressed with the mouth and eyes, mainly, but it's clear what the actor's feeling, that's for sure!

After selecting the actor's emotion, you then choose the action you want him to take while he speaks:

- Stand
- Jump
- Wave

- Shake
- Dance

Tip

You don't have to have your actors speak in every scene. Adding a dramatic pause or a quick scene in which one actor is shown with a different emotion before advancing to the next speaking scene can liven up the movie.

After you type what each actor says to the other for the scene, click "Next Scene," and the movie advances. For each scene, you need to make the same decisions:

- ◆ Camera angle
- ◆ Dialogue
- ◆ Emotion
- ◆ Action

You can shoot up to 15 different scenes for each movie, or you can shoot less. How many you need depends on how detailed your story line is and how much each character has to say to the other.

When you finish, it's time to save the movie and sit back and watch.

Warning

It's easy to forget to save your movie if you get called away or distracted, but if you don't click "Save" before exiting, all the work on your movie will be lost. So, remember to click "Save"!

Showing Movies

When you finish directing, you'll be brought back to the computer screen where you started. Notice in the bottom-right corner that there is the option to Watch Old Movies. These are movies you previously created.

When you click that, you see the different titles of your movies, and you can choose which you want to watch right now. Click the name of the movie, and it starts to play automatically.

In addition to sharing your brilliant show with your friends and family, from time to time you will also have the chance to have your movie shown on Webkinz TV. Watch for a contest announcement that asks you to enter movies you created, and you might be a lucky winner.

Although your child did the work, his Webkinz gets all the credit.

Tip

Even though a movie might be finished, you can go back and add characters as you buy them from the W Shop. You can rework the same movie several times if you like or start fresh. It's up to you.

The Least You Need to Know

◆ You can make animated movies of up to 15 scenes in Webkinz World starring cute animal characters.

◆ To make movies, you first need to buy the Webkinz Studio, which costs 1,000 KinzCash in the W Shop.

◆ Making a movie involves hiring actors, choosing background music, scenery, writing dialogue, and selecting different camera angles for each scene.

◆ You can use the basic actors and scenery that come with the studio, or you can buy additional actors and backgrounds in the W Shop.

◆ After you create a movie, you can watch it on screen and enter it in upcoming contests for a chance of having it appear on Webkinz TV. Watch the Newz for contest announcements.

Chapter 7

Cooking and Socializing

In This Chapter

◆ Mixing up delicious dishes

◆ Competing in cooking tournaments

◆ Testing Webkinz® recipes

◆ Webkinz parties on and offline

Two great activities are cooking and having friends over, and Webkinz makes it possible to do both. Your child can stir up proven recipes online or make up her own using Webkinz appliances and food. Or she can whip up some new flavor combinations in your kitchen by following Webkinz cookbooks.

Another activity your child can do online or off is to host a party, inviting friends over for some Webkinz fun. The offline variety certainly takes more planning and oversight, and online gatherings make it possible to hang out with friends from all over the world. Maybe they'll even offer to help clean up!

The Webkinz Kitchen

Webkinz World provides all the ingredients you need to do some serious virtual cooking. You can buy the food, appliances, and cookbooks at the W Shop and then either cook, blend, or grill up some tasty treats for your pet to enjoy.

Tested and Proven Recipes

Until you've purchased a stove, cauldron, barbeque, sandwich maker, or blender, however, you can't start whipping up any dishes for your animal. Each of these appliances can be bought in the W Shop's Kitchen and Bathroom category. You then move them into your pet's room for some gourmet activity.

With a blender, you can mix up some yummy concoctions, like fruit smoothies, dips, and salsa. To operate the blender, which is in My Room, move your pet so that it is standing next to the blender, and then click on the blender so that it opens a new computer screen.

According to Grant

"Blending foods together is pretty fun, but I usually end up making Gak. I don't try to make Gak, but that's just what I get with the foods I mix together."

You then see three circles, or bowls, which are where you're going to place up to three ingredients you want to mix together. Simply drag the food from your dock up into the circles and then click on "Blend." In just a few seconds, you'll have a new taste sensation.

You're given a recipe for a Strawberry Smoothie with the blender, along with several other names of dishes, but no hints on what are in them. That's for you to figure out.

The process of cooking with a stove, cauldron, or barbeque is much the same. Start up the appliance, choose the food to be combined, and see what happens when they're cooked by your Webkinz.

For guidance in possible dishes, you can purchase cookbooks written specifically for your type of appliance. That is, there is a cookbook for the blender titled *Totally Blendin'*, a cookbook titled *Simply Delicious* for the stove, and *The Art of Sandwiching* for the sandwich maker.

> **Keep It Simple**
>
> Make sure you buy the right cookbook for the right cookware in Webkinz World. The recipes have all been developed specifically for a particular appliance, which means you can't use stove recipes for the blender or vice versa. It just won't turn out well.

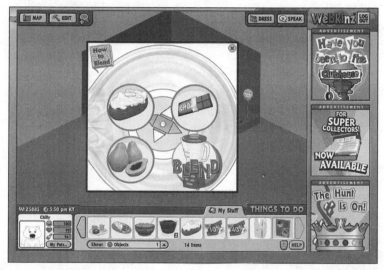

It's fun to see what new recipe you can invent by blending different foods together. But don't be frustrated if all you make is Gak—it can still be nutritious.

Figuring Out Secret Recipes

There are also named dishes that contain a certain combination of ingredients that your child can attempt to figure out. These are secret recipes that take time to break down into their raw materials.

For example, Plymouth Veggie Parfait consists of a pumpkin, baked potato, and peas whipped up in the blender. Or mix cookies, bananas, and ice cream on the stove to create Cookie Tornado. Baked beans, cheeses, and pancakes cooked on the sandwich maker, on the other hand, create bean burritos.

You can learn new recipes for the Chef's Challenge by watching the Chef Gazpacho show on a TV in your pet's room.

Webkinz Chef Challenge

A fun way to apply your knowledge of Webkinz recipes is by competing in the Webkinz Chef Challenge game in the Tournament Arena.

Just like the real television show, you and an opponent battle it out for chef supreme by whipping up interesting three-ingredient dishes.

The object of Chef Challenge is to create dishes that the three judges will prefer over your opponent. You're given a name of a dish and a selection of six ingredients, and you choose three to mix together to form the dish. The three judges then taste the dish and give you comments and a score. The highest score, between you and your opponent, wins the game.

While you're playing, it's always fun to click on "KinzChat," in the bottom-left corner of the screen and choose a saying to psych out your opponent—something like "I'm the master of the kitchen" always works.

 Tip

Pay attention to the judges' comments to learn their personal likes and dislikes. This can help you win later rounds. For example, if you know one hates blueberry cheesecake, don't use that as one of your ingredients. Use one the judge likes instead.

Unless you know the secret ingredients for the specific dish mentioned, you just have to guess what would be in something called Scrombled Flippy Flappers or Yumble Numblies.

The player with the highest score after three rounds wins and receives 30 KinzCash®. The opponent wins 10.

According to Grant

"You can do an Internet search to find websites that list the secret recipes and what are in them, so you have a better chance of winning Chef Challenge."

Throwing Webkinz Parties

Despite the many safety barriers to keep children on Webkinz safe, it is still possible to become acquainted with other Webkinz owners. You're not exactly friends in that you have no idea who they are, where they live, or anything particularly personal, but you can learn their pet's name and add them to your friends list.

One of the ways to get to know them a little is by hosting a party in your Webkinz's home, where you can spend some time with the folks you've met in Webkinz World.

Virtual Parties

Hosting a party in Webkinz World is a lot like hosting a party at home, where you choose a date and time for your get-together, send out invitations, and wait for friends to show up. Fortunately, online, the time frame is compressed—announcing a party the day before is perfectly fine when a real-life party might require a 3-week notice.

According to Grant

"To have a fun Webkinz party in Webkinz World, invite everyone in your friends list to come to your room. You can serve them food from the refrigerator in your room and cook some fun recipes while they're there."

The basic task with an online party is letting everyone you've met on Webkinz World know that they're invited to come check out and hang out in your pet's room at a particular date and time. You also need to specify which color zone to meet in, because you all need to be in the same zone to receive an invitation to enter your room.

When the date and time arrive, turn on the "Power" button on your cell phone and then systematically invite friends who pop up in green to join you in your room.

Warning

So many kids are hosting online Webkinz parties that it's now common for virtual goody bags to be distributed, including products purchased at the W Shop. If you decide to hold one, you might want to stock up on some small sale items before having people over.

In-Person Parties

While online Webkinz parties are hot, the in-person shindig might be even more exciting for those lucky enough to be invited.

Keep It Simple

If your child wants a Webkinz party, but you don't want to host it at home, look for a local Webkinz retailer who might already have a Webkinz party package available. Planet Make Believe in Akron, Ohio, for example, hosts such parties, providing everything you need for a big in-store bash.

As the popularity of Webkinz has skyrocketed, more children are having Webkinz parties, mainly for birthday celebrations. Although there are many possible activities and scenarios for such a party, some of the best items and ideas we found include the following:

◆ Send out Webkinz-themed printed invitations found online.

◆ Create a poster with the party activities and times listed, just like in Today's Activities.

◆ Give a Webkinz or Lil' Kinz® animal to each guest. Allow a 5-minute trading period when kids can swap.

◆ Make up a Wheel of Wow with miniprizes as a party activity.

◆ Fill a gumball machine with gumballs and have the kids guess how many gumballs are in it.

◆ Create games that mimic the games in the Arcade, such as Quizzy's Word Challenge, by giving out boards and tiles for party-goers to use in making words.

◆ Set up an art project where the kids make a small accessory for their new pets.

◆ Have a cooking activity where the kids make a secret Webkinz recipe or try to guess the ingredients in a premade dish by tasting it.

◆ Bake a cake in the shape of a big W and cover it with M&Ms or Skittles to look like the rainbow W.

◆ Have a gem hunt where the kids look for treasures using clues in different rooms of the house—or outdoors. Then they can trade them in for a prize or keep them.

Tip

Some Webkinz retailers host their own parties, which are actually activity hours, where children can enjoy Webkinz-related crafts and games at the store for a flat fee.

◆ Make minirooms out of cardboard boxes and provide furniture and decorations for the kids to decorate their houses, just like in Webkinz World—construction paper for wallpaper, fabric for window curtains and bedspreads, and child-size wood furniture or cardboard shaped into beds and chairs.

The Least You Need to Know

◆ You can buy cooking appliances for your pet to use in making tasty dishes in their room, as well as cookbooks for cooking tips.

◆ Webkinz Chef Challenge is a tournament game that involves using three ingredients to make the tastiest concoction in the hopes of beating a chef opponent.

◆ The name of the dish you're asked to make in Chef Challenge is often a combination of words that hint at the ingredients used.

◆ A Webkinz party can be hosted online or offline (in-person).

◆ Online parties involve inviting all the people in your friends list over to your pet's home at a particular day and time.

◆ Offline parties are usually birthday celebrations involving all things Webkinz—animals, activities, and recipes.

Chapter 8

Webkinz Trading Cards

In This Chapter

- ◆ Collecting Webkinz® cards
- ◆ Playing games
- ◆ Earning freebies
- ◆ Online trading cards

Webkinz Trading Cards come in two varieties: virtual and paper. Playing Webkinz Trading Challenge in the Tournament Arena requires no physical cards, though the paper cards allow kids to play several in-person card games, such as Challenge and Mix n' Match.

This chapter introduces the trading cards and explains how children can play with them.

The Ins and Outs of Trading Cards

Introduced in mid-2007, the first set of Webkinz trading cards consists of 80 base cards, 15 Challenge cards, eight Curio Shop Curiosities cards, and eight Webkinz Doodlez cards. More will be added in the future.

The colorful cards are sold in packs of six—five trading cards and one feature code card—for around $3 each.

Webkinz Trading Cards are a hot commodity and provide another way for children to connect with Webkinz in the real world.

The cards can be collected and traded with friends or used for playing games.

Collecting Cards

One way to play with the cards is to try and collect all 111 of the original set. You can do this by buying more card packs and by trading with friends, giving away multiples of cards you already have in exchange for cards you don't yet have.

Keep It Simple

Each box of 36-card packs that retailers receive to sell contains one card pack that has a code for a free Webkinz pet inside.

Each card has an identifier down the left side of the card that tells you what it is—these are called Traits, which include pet, character, item, and host, for example. And there is also a block of text at the bottom of the card that tells you more about the person, pet, or thing shown.

Base Cards

The first set of cards Ganz, the creators of Webkinz, introduced consisted of 80 base cards—the cards you use to play games.

Base cards form the core deck used to play games.

Featuring pictures of Webkinz pets, such as the Gold and White Cat; items, such as food you can buy in the W Shop; Arcade games, such as Candy Bash; characters, such as Webkinz host Ms. Birdy; as well as recipes, such as for Zazzeloop Soup, the base cards compose the core cards in the set.

> **Tip**
>
> Some base cards have a special symbol on them that means they can also be used as an action type of card. The symbol is a red circle with a gold lightning bolt through it. If you see that on a card, you can use it either way—as a base card or an action card.

Action Cards

Action cards let you do things when it's your turn, such as choosing a pet card in the discard pile and putting it into your hand or winning a challenge instantly. Each card has a picture and a block of text that tells you what to do if you decide to use it.

After you do it, you put the card in the discard pile during the game. (We'll tell you more about how to play a Challenge game in a minute.)

Action cards are easily distinguishable by a red border and the word Action in the upper-left corner.

Challenge Cards

Challenge cards show the challenges that players must complete to win the game. To win, you must finish four challenges.

Challenge cards are green, rather than blue, and are marked with the words Webkinz Challenge! on the front.

Each Challenge card has a name, such as Zacky's Quest, and a description of what you must do and what you earn as a result. The challenge, or what you must do, is noted with two small flags. The reward, or what you receive, has a small gold trophy to its left.

After you successfully complete a fourth challenge, you win.

Collectible Cards

Some cards are interesting to look at and collect, but they aren't used to play any games. These include Curio Shop Curiosities cards, which are foil cards that tell you the history of eight special items, one per card.

Another collectible card type is Webkinz Doodlez, which are foil cards showing sketches of characters you see in Webkinz World. You also learn a little more about how they were developed. Like the Curiosities cards, these are for collecting only, not for play.

Playing Games

Although Webkinz trading cards are fun to collect and trade, you can also use them to play a fun game called Webkinz Challenge. Or you can play Mix and Match, another card game, or Go Fish, an old favorite.

Webkinz Challenge

The object of Webkinz Challenge is to be the first player to complete a total of four Challenges.

To play, you first need to download and print out the Challenge board, which is available at www.webkinz.com/TCG_downloads.html. You can print it out on 11 × 17-inch paper, or you can print out two 8.5 × 11-inch sheets and tape them together.

The play mat helps show which challenges are available and where the various discard piles are.

To play the Challenge game, you first need to have 50 base cards and at least 7 Challenge cards. You can play with two or more people, but for every additional player beyond two, you need three more Challenge cards per player. So if you have two players, you only need seven Challenge cards, but if you have three players, you need 10 Challenge cards, and if you have four players, you need 13. You can have more than four players, too; you just need to keep adding Challenge cards to make it work.

Keep It Simple

If you ever run out of cards in the deck, just shuffle the cards from the discard pile and make a new deck to draw from.

Start by deciding who goes first. Then choose a dealer and deal out five cards from the deck to each player. The dealer takes the top three cards from the deck of Challenge cards and lays them face up on the play mat so that everyone can see them. These are what you want to complete as soon as possible.

Next, you start taking turns. When it is his or her turn, each player can do one of the following:

- Pick up the top card of the deck and put it into his or her hand.

- Discard a card into the discard pile and pick up the top two cards from the deck.

- Try to complete a Challenge.

- Play an Action card from his or her hand.

To play an Action card, say "I'm playing an Action" and show the card to everyone. Then do what the card says and discard the card in the discard pile.

Likewise, to attempt a Challenge, say "I'm attempting a Challenge" and tell the other players which Challenge you're going to do. Then do what the Challenge says and discard any cards into the discard pile.

Warning

If you complete a Challenge but you can't get your reward because the card you've been awarded isn't available, you simply do not get a prize. You still keep the Challenge card, however.

If you successfully complete a Challenge, pick up the card and put it in front of you so everyone knows you have completed it. Afterward, take the top card from the Challenge pile and place it in the empty Challenge spot.

After a player has had his turn, the player to his right goes next. The first person to complete four Challenges wins the game.

Building a Personal Challenge Deck

For even more fun playing Challenge, work on creating your own personal deck of trading cards that you use to play against other Webkinz owners. Go head-to-head to see who can win Challenges first.

To build a personal deck, you must do the following:

◆ Compile a deck of at least 30 cards.

◆ Make sure you do not have more than three of any one card.

◆ Choose five different Challenges you can complete using your personal deck.

To play a Challenge game with a personal deck, place your deck in front of you. You draw from your deck and your opponent draws from his personal deck. Shuffle your five Challenge cards together with your opponent's cards. You create your own discard pile, and your opponent does likewise—you don't discard into his pile, only to yours.

Warning

To avoid disagreements over who owns which cards, consider putting your child's initials in a corner of her cards to tell them apart from her friends' cards.

Mix n' Match

Another game the folks at Webkinz created is Mix n' Match, which is for two to four players. You need 40 base cards but no Action or Challenge cards.

To start, choose someone to go first. The dealer shuffles the deck and deals seven cards to each player, placing the remaining cards in the center of the table, with the top one turned over next to the deck. That is the discard pile.

Players then take turns. During their turn, players can do one of the following:

◆ Discard a card from their hand and pick up a new one from the top of the deck.

◆ Place a card from their hand on the bottom of the deck, face down, and pick up the top card on the discard pile.

◆ Put down a *mixed* or *matched* set of four cards and then draw three cards from the top of the deck.

A *mixed* set consists of four cards where none of the traits match, such as a pet, host, item, and arcade. A *matched* set of cards has at least one shared trait, such as all food or all characters.

The first player to lay down her fourth mixed or matched set wins.

Go Fish

You can play Go Fish with Webkinz cards just as you do with traditional playing cards. Two players can play, and you need 11 sets of four matching cards. You don't use Action or Challenge cards in Go Fish.

Players are dealt six cards. They take turns asking the others if they have a card like one they have in their hand. So, for example, if one player has a Black Lab card, he would ask the other player for all her Black Lab cards. The other player then has to give all her Black Lab cards, not just one. If the player then has four cards, he can lay them down in front of him as a "book."

If the other player does not have any of the cards requested, she says "Go Fish," and the player asking for the cards takes the top card from the deck and adds it to his hand.

The first player to lay down her sixth book wins the game. If any player runs out of cards, the game ends, and the player with the most books wins, even if she doesn't yet have six.

Feature Code Cards

Every trading-card pack contains one feature code card that has the Challenge game rules on one side and at least one feature code—but maybe as many as five—plus another code for a free virtual trading card pack to be used in Webkinz World.

Feature Codes

Each pack of trading cards contains one card listing the rules of the Challenge game on one side and feature codes on the other. Feature codes are a series of letters and numbers that you type on the screen at the Code Shop in Webkinz World.

With each code entered, you receive a random prize ranging from KinzCash, furniture, food, coupons, or maybe even a rare or exclusive item.

According to Grant

"I got one feature card that had four codes on it. I entered them and got lots of KinzCash® and a cool TV for my pets."

Virtual Trading Cards

Each card pack also comes with one virtual pack of Webkinz trading cards, which can be unlocked at the Code Shop. After you enter the code for a virtual card pack in the Code Shop, click "Unlock," and a picture of a card pack appears in your dock.

To see what is in it, you need to go to My Room and then drag it into the room. You'll need to buy the Webkinz Trading Card Series 1 Binder from the Games section of the W Shop, which costs 100 KinzCash. By dragging the binder into your room, you can then see all the virtual cards you now own.

After you collect all of them, you can win other virtual prizes. Just click "Unlocked Prizes" on your binder to see what cards you still need.

The Least You Need to Know

◆ Webkinz trading cards can be collected and traded with friends or used to play games like Challenge, Mix n' Match, and Go Fish.

◆ Each pack of cards includes a feature card containing between one to five codes you can enter in the Code Shop to earn KinzCash, rare items, food, coupons, and items available only through these codes.

◆ You need at least 50 base cards and at least seven Challenge cards to play Webkinz Challenge.

◆ There is a downloadable play mat to help you learn how to play Challenge.

◆ You can build your own personal deck of trading cards, which you can use to play against other Webkinz owners with their own decks.

◆ In addition to Challenge, you can play Mix n' Match or Go Fish with your trading cards.

9

FAQs (Frequently Asked Questions)

In This Chapter

◆ Answers to common questions

◆ Little-known shortcuts

◆ Troubleshooting techniques

◆ Other information sources

Even parents with savvy Webkinz® owners at home are bound to come across a how-to question or situation that needs addressing. And when that situation arises, you want to resolve it immediately for your children. Because that's what parents do—they offer solutions.

We put together some answers to questions that are bound to crop up at some point, in the hopes this chapter will be a quick reference guide for you.

Taking Care of Your Pet

Because the care and feeding of Webkinz animals is a core component of Webkinz World, it's good to know how best to care for the little cuties.

What Does the Happiness, Health, and Hunger Meter Mean?

The happiness, health, and hunger meter in the bottom-left corner of your screen gives you an immediate sense of how your pet feels and whether anything is amiss. Although pets are generally always happy, unless you haven't visited them in a while, their health and hunger measures can drop if they aren't fed or if they aren't put to bed when you leave Webkinz World. They get worn out.

What Do I Do If My Webkinz Gets Sick?

If you forget to feed your pet for a few days or you keep it active for long periods of time, it'll become ill. To find out what's wrong, you can visit the Clinic, which is on the Things to Do menu bar. It tells you what you need to do to bring your Webkinz back to good health, which might include buying some medicine.

Can My Webkinz Die?

No, your pet can get sick, but it won't die. However, if you go more than 90 days without logging in, your account will be deactivated.

How Can I Get Food to Feed My Pet?

The Webkinz money, called KinzCash®, you get when you adopt your pet is for feeding and caring for your pet. You can spend that cash at the W Store, which sells a wide range of food in its Food section.

To buy food, click the food you want, click "Add to Cart," and then click "Buy"; it appears in your dock at the bottom of the screen.

How Do I Feed My Pet?

You can feed your pet in two ways; you can drag food from the dock to the left and directly onto the little picture of your pet, or you can drag it from your dock and onto your pet while it is in its room.

What Do I Need to Care for My Pet?

Just like humans, your Webkinz needs rest at night. Every time you leave your pet's room, be sure and put your Webkinz in its bed so that it can sleep.

Bathing your pet is another way to help keep it healthy and happy. To do that, however, you need to buy a bathtub at the W Shop and put it in your pet's room. When you click it, a new screen opens up, and you can scrub your pet with a sponge and soap. You also see its health meter improve when you take it out of the tub.

How Do I Talk to My Pet?

When you're in your pet's room, you see a button in the bottom-left corner of the computer screen—Speak to Pet. When you click that blue button, you can Say, Ask, or Rap with your pet. When you Say something, you tell your pet something. With Ask, you can ask your pet something. And Rap let's you talk more conversationally.

Your Pet's Room

In addition to sheltering your Webkinz, your pet's room (My Room) is also where you can play together, talk, and invite friends over.

How Do I Add Wall Color or Furniture?

First, you need to buy the items you want to have in your room, which are sold at the W Shop. You can buy paint for your walls, carpet for your floor, furniture, appliances—such as refrigerators—windows, TVs, and more.

After you purchase them, they appear in your dock, down at the bottom of your screen. To move them into your room, you drag them up and place them where you'd like them to be within the room. You see squares outlined as you move the item in—green means you can place the item there, and red means you can't. (If you want to put a window on the floor, you can't.)

I Have Too Many Rooms. How Do I Sell Some Back.

You can sell food and other items you purchase or receive back to the W Shop by clicking the "W Shop" and then clicking "Sell."

However, you can't sell back or delete rooms you no longer want. You can redecorate them, but you can't get rid of them. That's why you are asked a couple of times if you really, really want to add another room when you're in the process of adding one.

What Is an Exclusive Item?

An exclusive item is a special product for your Webkinz's room that is available only when you do something, such as buy more Webkinz or win it through a contest.

What Items Can My Pet Play With and Which Are for Decoration?

When you go to the W Shop to make a purchase, click the category of product you want to look at, such as Furniture or Toys and Books.

As you click on each item within that category, a little picture pops up along with a description of it and a price. If the product is interactive, meaning that you and your pet can do something more than just look at it, you'll see a blue semicircle with the word "Interactive" in the lower-right corner of the picture. In the description of the product, too, it says whether the item is for decoration only, such as sofas and chairs, or whether it is interactive.

How Can I Move My Pet from Room to Room?

One way is to click the square leading into another room, and your pet will walk there.

Another way is to click "Map" and then "Jump"; then click the picture of the room you want to immediately go to. This way is quicker if you have several rooms in your house.

Can I Invite a Friend Over?

To invite a friend over to play in your Webkinz's room, first go to your room. Then click the phone in the lower-right corner of the screen. When it pops up, click "Power" so that it turns on. You see a list of people who are on your Friends list. Any of the names of your friends who have a green smiley face next to them are people who are currently in Webkinz World and could come visit. If a name has a red face next to it, that means they are not around. A yellow face means they are online but don't want to be disturbed at the moment—maybe they're in a big tournament and don't want to interrupt their playing.

When you find a friend who is online, click her name and then click the word "Invite." She receives a message on her computer screen that asks if she wants to come visit your Webkinz. If she does, you hear a high voice saying "Yoohoo," and your friend appears at your Webkinz's door.

When you finish playing and you want your friend to go home, click the button on the screen that says "Send all friends home."

How Do I Send a Friend a Note?

Sending a note is easy through KinzPost, the Webkinz postal service.

Click "KinzPost" on the Things to Do menu and then click "Send a Note." You decide who you want to send a note to and then select the message you want to send. Using simple stationery costs just 1 KinzCash, but if you want to get fancy and use other stationery, it can cost a lot more.

After you press "Send," the message is sent, and the next time your friend visits her room, she sees that she has mail.

How Do I Know When I Have Mail?

When you visit My Room and see a little picture of an envelope on the left side of the screen, click it, and it will automatically open. You can then read the note from your friend.

Can I Send a Friend KinzCash?

No, you can't send or lend a friend money, but you can send them a gift through KinzPost, which is under the Things to Do menu bar. Simply click "KinzPost" and then click whether you want to send a note—which costs at least 1 KinzCash—or send a gift—which costs at least 15 KinzCash per item.

If you decide to send a gift, click the friend you want to send an item to and then drag something from your dock up into the packing box. You also have to decide whether to pay extra for a special box and wrapping paper, as well as a note to go along with the gift.

You can send up to three items to each friend per day. Webkinz sets this limit as a safety precaution in case someone gets your password and wants to take your belongings.

What Are Growing Gardens?

You can decide to decorate an outdoor room with decorative plants and trees, or you can plant a garden with fruit and vegetables that will grow—Growing Gardens. After you've taken care of them for 7 days, you can harvest the food and feed it to your Webkinz.

Or if that's not appealing, just buy plants that don't need care.

Navigating Webkinz World

Webkinz World is so big that it might take a while to find your way around. Here are some commonly asked questions to help you show your child around.

How Can I Earn More KinzCash?

You can earn more KinzCash in Webkinz World in many ways. The best way is to answer Quizzy's questions, found in the Things to Do area, because you earn 5 KinzCash for each correct answer. But you also earn KinzCash for playing Arcade games and competing in tournaments; although, it might just take longer.

Other ways to earn KinzCash include spinning the Wheel of Wow once a day; going to the Wishing Well once a day; doing the Gem Hunt at the Curio Shop once a day; taking a job at the Employment Office, which you can do once every 8 hours; taking surveys, which are in the Contact Us section of the *Newz* page; and clicking "I love my Webkinz" once a day at the My Pets KinzCare page.

There are also other opportunities to earn extra KinzCash or to win fun prizes listed in Today's Activities. Make sure you check that regularly.

Are the Gems in the Mines Always in the Same Locations?

No. The gems are randomly moved after every mining session, so they are rarely in the same place, but they do stay within the same mine.

How Do I Earn a Webkinz Crown of Wonder?

You can ask Arte, the owner of the Curio Shop, to make a Crown of Wonder for you after you collect all 30 of the gems in the mines. You can then keep the crown or sell it back.

Why Does Arte Have a Tip Jar on His Counter?

You can decide to give Arte a tip for his service by clicking the "Tip Jar." Then click the amount of KinzCash you want to give him. After several tips, Arte might tell you about an upcoming rare item or tell you when it will become available.

How Do You Play a Game in the Arcade?

Each game in the Arcade, which you get to by clicking the "Arcade" button from Things to Do, offer instructions on how to play. Some also offer a Show Me button, which is like a mini tutorial that explains how the game works.

How Can I Get a High Score?

High scores earned for Arcade games are tracked monthly and reset at the beginning of each month, so your best chance of winning the coveted high score position is at the beginning of the month.

Daily high scores are updated throughout the day but sometimes don't get posted until the end of the day.

How Do I Know if My Friend is in Webkinz World?

You know friends are in Webkinz World if you turn your phone on, which is down in the right corner of My Room and you see the little face next to a friend's name is green and smiling. If it's yellow, the friend is online but doesn't want to be disturbed—maybe they're in the middle of a big game—and if it's red, they're not around.

You might need to check the different colored zones to learn whether your friend is in another part of Webkinz World.

What Is a Great Play and How Can I Earn One?

A Great Play is an Arcade game score that Webkinz feels is noteworthy. The company announces it in the Arcade Achievements page under Scores and Achievements.

Solutions for Technical Issues

Sometimes, Webkinz World has technical difficulties. Here's what to do if you encounter problems.

I Can't Find the Log In Button on My Screen; What's Wrong?

Sometimes, Webkinz World closes temporarily for maintenance and upgrades. This usually happens late at night. During that time, you can't enter. There is usually a note explaining that the site is closed at the moment.

Is There a Manual I Can Read?

Other than this book, you can also click the "Help" function in the bottom-right corner of every page for guidance. You can also flip open the Webkinz guide that is in your room, which offers helpful hints and advice. Or you can go to the Contact Us window on the *Newz* page and enter a question there. You receive a KinzPost note in your room within 24 hours with the answer.

Do I Have to Set Up a New Account If I Get Another Webkinz?

No. It's actually better if you keep all your pets registered to the same account. That way they can share rooms, and you can easily care for them from one screen, under My Pets on the Things to Do menu.

Each additional Webkinz you register earns you increasing amounts of KinzCash. The first earns you 2,000 KinzCash to start, then 3,000 for the second, and so on. Each new pet also extends your annual access by a year from the latest registration. So if you have 9 months left on your registration and you register a new pet, your registration is extended to a year from that date.

Everything in My Dock Is Gone. What Happened?

Chances are that the food, furniture, and clothing you had in your dock are in storage, so click the "Items in Storage" button above your dock, and everything should reappear in the boxes below.

The Least You Need to Know

◆ Webkinz World provides answers to many questions about the site both in the Webkinz Guide in your pet's room and through the Help function.

◆ If you can't find an answer in this book or in the Help section, you can send a question through the Contact Us page.

◆ Sometimes, Webkinz World is shut down overnight for maintenance, but it usually reopens the next day.

◆ If you don't do anything for several minutes at the site, you get a message asking if you want to remain connected. If you don't respond, you will be automatically logged out.

Appendix A

Webkinz and Lil' Kinz

New Webkinz® and Lil' Kinz® pets are introduced every few months. As of Summer 2007, this is the current collection.

Alley Cat

Basset Hound

Beagle

Black and White Cat

Black Bear

Black Lab

Bull Dog

Bull Frog

Cheeky Cat

Cheeky Dog

Cheeky Monkey

Chihuahua

Chocolate Lab

Clydesdale

Cocker Spaniel

Cow

Dalmatian

Elephant

Frog

Gold and White Cat

Golden Retriever

Googles

Gorilla

Gray and White Cat

Hippo

Horse

Husky

Koala

Leopard

Lion

Love Puppy

Monkey

Panda

Pegasus

Persian Cat

Pig

Pink Pony

Pink Poodle

Polar Bear

Poodle

Pug

Rabbit

Raccoon

Sherbet Bunny

Spotted Frog

St. Bernard

Tiger

Tree Frog

Unicorn

White Terrier

Yorkie

The following Webkinz are also available as Lil' Kinz:

Alley Cat

Basset Hound

Black and White Cat

Black Bear

Chihuahua

Cocker Spaniel

Cow

Elephant

Frog

Gold and White Cat

Golden Retriever

Gorilla

Gray and White Cat

Hippo

Horse

Lion

Monkey

Panda

Persian Cat

Pig

Poodle

Pug

Rabbit

St. Bernard

Tiger

Tree Frog

Unicorn

White Terrier

Yorkie

Appendix B

Where to Buy Webkinz

Finding Webkinz® pets in stock at retailers in the United States has been a parent's biggest challenge, really. Sure, learning the ins and outs takes time, but tracking down a Webkinz animal has proven even harder at times.

In general, Webkinz are stocked by smaller toy stores, gift shops, and Hallmark stores nationally. You can also find them at Amazon.com and on eBay, though expect to pay more online because there are shipping costs.

For a complete list of stores carrying Webkinz, go to www. webkinz.com and click on Store Locator. You'll be asked to provide your country, state, and city. Then a window will pop up providing all the names, addresses, and phone numbers of retailers in your town that stock them.

We strongly suggest you call first to make sure the store has what you're looking for before you head out. The list will certainly reduce your search time by knowing which stores do and don't carry Webkinz.

Gem Hunt Hints

If you know where to look, it's a little easier to find specific gems you may need. Use this guide to track down elusive stones.

Each mine has a specific color gem buried in it, but there are a few extras of different colors, too.

Buried Bones Mine

- ◆ Where white gems are buried.
- ◆ The only place you'll find the Webkinz® Diamond.
- ◆ Aurora Rox is here.
- ◆ Pyramid Plunder is also here.

Barking Mad Mine

- ◆ Where yellow gems are buried.
- ◆ Teardrop Tower is here.
- ◆ Sea Stone is here.

Flea Floater Mine

◆ Where green gems are buried.

◆ Ember Amber is here.

◆ Volcano Viscose is here, too.

Howling Horse Mine

◆ Where blue gems are buried.

◆ The only place you'll find the Ocean Sapphire.

◆ Moss Marble is here.

◆ Cat's Eye Glint is here.

Muzzle Mouth Mine

◆ Where the red gems are buried.

◆ The only place you'll find the Ruby Red Heart.

◆ Unicorn Horn is here.

◆ Yum Zum Sparkle is also here.

Index

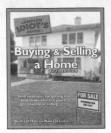

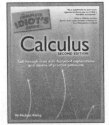